ADULTS
Only
TRAVEL

THE ULTIMATE GUIDE
to Romantic and Erotic Destinations

D1302205

THE ULTIMATE GUIDE
to Romantic and Erotic Destinations

SECOND EDITION
Revised

DAVID WEST AND LOUIS JAMES

Diamond Publishing

Diamond Publishing
A Division of Diamond Media Group L.L.C.
Copyright © 2003 Diamond Media Group and LouDak Media. All rights reserved.
Adults Only Travel™ is a trademark of Diamond Media Group.

ISBN 0-9712750-1-7

Cover Photo: Edmund Nagele, F.R.P.S.
Editor: Jana Nickel

We welcome your input. Please send any comments,
questions, criticisms, or contributions you may have to:

Diamond Publishing
3819 Rivertown Parkway
Suite 300 #202
Grandville, MI 49418
Email us at: info@adultsonlytravel.com

For additional information or to sign up for our free Adults Only Travel Bulletin
please visit our website at: www.adultsonlytravel.com.

Manufactured in the United States of America

Photo credits:
LaSOURCE, Rendezvous, LeSPORT, Runaway Hill Club/CPS Graphics, Swept Away
Negril, Natadola Beach Resort, The Caves Resort, Pleasure Cove Lodge, The Terra
Cotta Inn, Blue Bay Resorts, Caribbean Reef Club, Desert Shadows Inn Resort & Villas,
Patos Planet, Harmony Club, Galley Bay, Club Ambiance, Turtle Island, Strawberry
Hill Resort, Couples Negril, La Casa de los Suenos/Leticia Alarcon, Westwind Inn, Cliff
House, Holden House, Morningside Inn, Louis Ducharme/Ice Hotel Quebec Canada,
Villa Escondida, Endless Summer II, Star Clippers/Harvey Lloyd, Viking Exotic
Cruises, Cruising For Love, Castaways Travel, Argosy Cruises, Windstar
Cruises/Kanauer Johnston/Len Kaufman/Sandra Geldenhuys/J. Butchofsky -
Houser/Steve Schimmelman/Gerald Brimacombe/Gary Nolton, Nude Crewz Barebuns
Charter's, Free Land Marketing, AVN Adult Entertainment Expo, Nudes-A-Poppin,
Through Our Eyes Travel, Exotic Erotic Ball/Dave Patrick, Exotic Dancer Fan Fair,
European Body Painting Festival, The Sex Maniacs Ball, Mark R. Craven/Fetish Fantasy
Ball, Sybaris, Sea Mountain Ranch, 7 Palms.

*For all those who are open to new ideas,
fresh perspectives and never ending adventures.*

A Word of Thanks

It is impossible to research and compile the amount of information within this guide without the help and unwavering support of many people. So many gave of their time and knowledge that a full list of acknowledgment would cover more pages then we could realistically devote.

In particular, we would like to say thank-you to the many travel agents and industry professionals who were so generous with their years of hard earned knowledge. Many thanks to the managers and owners of the destinations who shared their time and expertise with us to help make this a much better guide.

Surrounding ourselves with wonderful people has not only made our life much easier, but a lot more fun as well. Thank-you so much to our amazing group of researchers who always help keep our spirits high. Special thanks to Debra and Elizabeth for their ongoing encouragement and support through all our travels together.

Contents

🌴 Resorts

🏠 Bed & Breakfasts, Villas and Inns

⛵ Cruises

👓 Hot Spots

Introduction

Imagine you and your partner relaxing in the sun with a tall glass of your favorite icy cold beverage. You're both luxuriating next to a pool that overlooks the ocean on your own private tropical island paradise. While softly talking to each other about your plans for an exciting evening together, the only other sound you hear is that of breaking waves in the near distance and the occasional sweet song of an exotic bird. There are no children in sight, leisurely or provocative activities await and a staff of seasoned professionals are available to cater to your every desire.

That's what this guide is all about! *Adults Only Travel* for romantic, childfree or erotic fun. While kids are great, there is a time and place for everything. When you are seeking a family vacation, it makes sense to seek out the best destinations that are devoted to family fun. On the other hand, there may be times when you strictly desire the company of other adults or the uninterrupted romantic possibilities with your partner. It's these times when you want the best in adult only travel.

With the many choices available in adult destinations today, it is very easy to quickly become overwhelmed searching for just the right spot. This guide has done the work for you! We have devoted a great deal of time to seek out and research what we felt are some of the most romantic, tantalizing and unique travel destinations around the world. They primarily cater to a mature, liberal-minded or adventurous adult. While we strived to include destinations that are adults only, there may be some that were too interesting to exclude but may choose to accept guests less than 18 years old. However, these few would still be considered adult focused destinations.

It is important to mention that none of the destinations featured in this guide paid anything to be included. They were chosen strictly because they offered a very different travel experience. You will notice throughout the guide that we have included destinations in many different budget ranges and tastes. Some are large all inclusive resorts, cruise lines etc., while others are small establishments and charters operated by the owners themselves. We did not include a destination only because it met a certain industry rating, but rather because of its uniqueness and romantic or erotic possibilities.

Everyone will have different preferences and levels of adventure they are willing to pursue. While every destination may not be right for you, we have provided such a wide variety that we are confident you will find something that will spark your imagination, and your desire to pack your bags and enjoy the trip of your dreams.

How this guide is organized:

This guide is divided into four primary sections. There are *Resorts; Bed & Breakfasts, Villas and Inns; Cruises;* and *Hot Spots.* Our goal was to include a wide variety of options for adults, but we also felt the need to make it extremely easy to navigate. Our guide allows you to read it from front to back or jump around to explore your favorite interests. Also, this is not a typical area guide that offers you every last detail about a specific region and area or the best time to go and what type of sun tan lotion you need to bring. Rather, you will be exposed to some of the most interesting adult destinations available throughout the world. At the same time, you will be getting enough of a feel for each so that you can investigate further if that is your desire. It is our hope that reading this guide will be a fun experience that lets your imagination run wild and prompts you to take advantage of some of the most unique destinations available.

Included is a small summary about each section of the guide so you can become more familiar with the type of destinations available within each category.

Resorts:

You will find enticing resorts within this section and they come in all flavors and sizes. Many are all inclusive including room, drinks, gourmet cuisine and various activities. All have something very unique in store for you, from large properties with hundreds of rooms and amenities galore, to smaller properties with fewer rooms and an abundance of personal care for its guests. Some of the resorts offer clothing optional opportunities as well. Nude beaches, nude volleyball, and clothing optional parties may peak your interest.

If baring it all is not your idea of a good time, there are just as many resorts that offer romantic or adventurous activities for those of us who like to keep our clothes on. Most offer free activities such as water sports, hiking, and bike trails. Many offer additional services for a small fee such as massage and sightseeing tour packages.

There are many fantastic resorts throughout the world that cater to an adult audience. From mild romance (if that's possible) to exotic adventure, you'll find it here in the *Resorts* section.

Bed & Breakfasts, Villas and Inns:

If it's charm, romance, intimacy and seclusion that you seek, then this is a section you'll love. Of the thousands of Bed and Breakfasts, Villas and Inns throughout the world, we strived to include some of the best in personal attention, unique and beautiful surroundings and romantic atmosphere. Tropical settings to northern wilderness and everything in between are what you will find as backdrops to these fantastic little pieces of paradise.

While there are many great features unique to each individual destination, one of the things you will find again and again is the level of personal attention. Most are owner operated and are a labor of love that you will notice right away. Secluded verandahs, private in-room jacuzzis, lavish facilities and an extremely accommodating staff are just some of the things awaiting you.

Every destination offers you the chance to escape and create the fantasy vacation you've always dreamed of. Some of the adult theme rooms you will encounter in this section will surely have you thinking about how soon you can take your next fantasy trip.

Cruises:

Nothing we can think of equals the true freedom you feel when you're aboard a cruise. Whether your preference is a large commercial liner, a tall sailing ship or a small charter with captain and crew, this is where you will find some of the best adult cruises available.

As you know, there are many cruises available, as well as some great guidebooks on conventional cruising. But what this section offers is much different. Following our guidelines for unique adult adventures, many of the cruises in this section are either nude or clothing optional, and most have the possibility of a much more private and romantic experience.

Nude cruising has long been a favorite among adventurous adults. And for good reason! Cruising in the buff provides adults with a chance to experience the exhilaration of being clothes free on the open water, try nude diving and snorkeling, or just working on an all over tan, all with other like-minded adults.

Maybe it's the large ships you're after. You will find large commercial ships provide amenities galore. Almost anything you can think of in the way of activities is here for your pleasure. The many people onboard give you unequaled socializing opportunities.

If you prefer the delights of a private cruising adventure, you can try one of the smaller charters. Most of these smaller charters can indulge your requests for a much more intimate experience. This is something not afforded to guests of the larger ships. You might like to try a secluded beach where you could enjoy a very private, romantic lunch for two. Almost anything imaginable can easily be arranged to suit your budget, tastes and fantasies.

There are also some very unique clothed cruises in this section with some that focus their attention solely on singles as well as a variety of other options. If you really want to experience a one-of-a-kind adult adventure, you owe it to yourself to try out one of these fabulous cruises at least once.

👓 Hot Spots:

Looking for a sexy, erotic or just plain wild time? How about some place out-of-the-ordinary? Have you ever thought of attending an adult expo where you can find the latest in adult products, toys and lingerie before they even become available on the market? Maybe partying at some of the most erotic balls and dances is your desire. Or you might have always wanted to take your relationship to new heights by chartering your very own private flight to join the mile high club. Perhaps you were looking for a place where you could get married in a hot air balloon or while bungee jumping in the buff! Of course, you don't have to wait to get married to indulge yourself.

This section is all about very unique and erotic adult events, and some out-of-the-ordinary spots that are really in a category all their own. Many of these wild events can be attended as a day or weekend getaway, or you could even plan a complete sexy vacation around any one of these *Hot Spots*. If you are seeking adult fun and excitement you will find some of the best here.

Additional Resources:

We have provided a *Resource* section in the back of the guide that lists many adult and clothing optional travel agencies.

Whether you choose to use one of these specialty agencies listed here or your own travel agent, we always recommend that where applicable you book your vacation through a reputable and friendly agent. They can usually find you a much better deal than you can find yourself, and a good agent will provide a level of knowledge and friendly service that will usually make your travels a much better experience.

Geographic Locations:

If you would like to locate a destination in a particular area of the world, you will find geographic locations of each destination in the back of the book within the index. Simply scan the geographic index listings and locate the destination and page you desire.

You will no doubt find some very unique and interesting adult destinations within this guide. Our hope is that they will spark your imagination as well as your desire for the best in romantic, childfree and erotic travels. Enjoy!

ADULTS *Only* TRAVEL

Resorts

LeSPORT

Castries, St. Lucia

Found on the Caribbean island of St. Lucia, LeSPORT is an all-inclusive resort with lavish, tropical grounds, Spanish-inspired architecture, and plenty of sunshine. Here, you'll find all the amenities of a typical island resort vacation combined with extensive spa services. Fitness classes, massage therapies, beauty treatments, relaxation therapies, and a variety of sports including tennis, fencing, archery and more, are all available on site. Best of all, almost all of these services are included in the price of your stay. Spend your morning using these pampering services before soaking up the island sun on the nude sunbathing deck. For the afternoon, lounge on the beach, try a sport on land or sea, or return to your room for a nap.

Guest rooms at the resort are housed in several different buildings and come in various sizes from garden rooms for singles to ocean front suites available with one or two bedrooms. All rooms are beautifully decorated with quality furnishings and offer air conditioning, direct dial phones, and a private bath with shower. Some rooms are also available with ocean views, balconies, and mini refrigerators.

For your dining pleasure, LeSPORT offers two main onsite restaurants, Cariblue and Tao. Cariblue offers breakfast and lunch buffets as well as a la carte dinner menu in a fairly casual setting. For a more refined dining experience, visit award-winning Tao for dinner. This upscale restaurant offers Pacific Rim/East-West Fusion style cuisine in a warm, intimate setting. Make your reservations early because Tao is extremely popular. There is also a small deli featuring light sandwiches and salads, and an onsite bar offering drink service and nightly dancing. Drink service is also available on the beach and by the pool.

LeSPORT

CONTACT:

WEBSITE:
www.lesport.com.lc

EMAIL:
sales@lesport.com.lc

PHONE:
758-450-8551 or 800-544-2883

FAX:
758-450-0368

ADDRESS:
LeSPORT
Cariblue Beach,
P.O. Box 437
Castries, St. Lucia,
West Indies

SERVICES: There are a vast number of services included in the price of your stay including holistic therapies, massage, relaxation classes, fitness classes, and land and water sports. For an additional fee, make use of the facility's boutique and salon.

DINING: Two main restaurants are available onsite. Cariblue offers break-fast and lunch buffets featuring healthy fare from around the world and an a la carte dinner menu. Sophisticated Tao is open only for dinner serving elegant Pacific Rim/East-West Fusion style cuisine. For a lighter, quicker meal, try The Deli for sandwiches and salads.

RATES: Rates per person per night are generally $500.00 to $800.00 and vary according to type of room and time of year. Call or visit their website's online booking page for current information.

Resorts

Getaway Sun Resort

Jalisco, Mexico

Located on the shores of Bahía de Banderas, one of Mexico's largest natural bays, the Getaway Sun Resort in Puerto Vallarta is one of the most romantic all-inclusive destinations on the Mexican Riviera. The resort is only a short walk from town where you'll enjoy the old town charm that Puerto Vallarta has to offer including cobblestone streets and a beachside boardwalk. With over 250 restaurants offering a variety of cuisine choices, enchanting day tours by both land and boat, short cruises to surrounding islands, and exciting night life at any one of the numerous downtown bars you will always have something to keep you occupied outside of your room

Getaway Sun Resort offers various room types. Each has air-conditioning, a ceiling fan, satellite TV, a direct dial telephone and a safety deposit box. The larger suites come with balconies and offer complete ocean view, while the other room types have a partial ocean view. The property is all-inclusive, so you get lots of amenities and all your meals included in the price. Between meals enjoy healthy snacks, fruit juices and soft drinks, all complimentary. If you're looking for something a little more adventurous, check out Getaway's sister resort scheduled to open in November of 2003. Lifestyles Sun Resorts is also all-inclusive and offers a more hedonistic atmosphere for couples that want to fulfill their fantasies.

Honeymooners don't forget to bring your marriage certificate to get a free upgrade to a luxury room. They'll also have a bottle of sparkling wine and a bowl of fruit waiting in your room.

SERVICES: Getaway Sun Resort offers plenty to keep you occupied with two swimming pools, an exercise room with steam bath and jacuzzi, three restaurants offering 24-hour food service, tennis courts, three bars, an outdoor theatre with nightly shows, a ping-pong table and lush gardens. There are also a variety of non-motorized water sports including a wind glider, kayaks and boogie boards. Or simply enjoy the tranquility of watching the sun sink by the pool at Arthur's Sunset Bar.

DINING: You won't go hungry at Getaway Sun Resort. There are four restaurants including an "a la carte" steak house (requires a reservation) and breakfast buffet. Plus there is a lunch and light dinner beachside snack bar. You can waste away the evening dancing and sipping on your favorite while listening to music at either the beach or tequila bar.

RATES: Room rates are from $130.00 to $145.00 single occupancy and $98.00 to $113.00 double occupancy. Extra person is $103.00. All room rates are per night and also include domestic and selected international drinks. Room types vary allowing either two or three adults maximum occupancy per room. Getaway Sun Resort does not allow anyone under 18 years of age.

Jules' Undersea Lodge

Key Largo, Florida

Do you dream of Atlantis? Do you fantasize about what it would be like to be a mermaid or to be with a mermaid? Imagine you could live underwater with all the magic of the sea for just a little while. At Jules' Undersea Lodge, this seemingly impossible fantasy comes true. Jules' is a submarine facility resting 21 feet below the surface in the Florida Keys. To reach the lodge, you have to be able to dive. The establishment offers short diving classes at a discount for anyone visiting the lodge that's not already certified. Day trips to the undersea vessel are available, but for the most romantic experience, you'll want to stay overnight. Rent the entire facility and you and your partner can rule over your own underwater kingdom for the night.

The lodge consists of two, cylindrical rooms that have been outfitted with everything necessary to keep you comfortable for days on end. There are two bedrooms, a common sitting area, a fully stocked kitchen, and two 42 inch, round windows to serve as your link to the abundance of aquatic life just outside. The sub also has air-conditioning, hot showers, a TV and VCR, and mood music for your enjoyment. For your safety, conditions inside the sub are constantly monitored from a station above. Dinner is prepared by a "mer-chef" who dives down to you to create a memorable gourmet dinner for two. You can dive around the sub as often as you like and a romantic evening dive is the perfect end to the day. Back inside the sub, you have the total privacy needed to let your watery fantasies unfold.

Wake in the morning to see the lagoon outside teeming with ocean life. Soon your chef will return to make a delicious breakfast for you before you start another day of adventure.

Resorts

And if you're thinking about getting married, why not tie the knot in the world's only underwater hotel. Jules' offers a complete wedding package that includes romantic music, a cake, fresh flowers, a notary who dives down to perform the wedding and use of your personal "mer-chef" that will prepare your gourmet meals. Extra guests can attend the ceremony for only $60 per person. An extended honeymoon package is also available.

Jules' Undersea Lodge

CONTACT:

WEBSITE:
www.jul.com

EMAIL:
info@jul.com

PHONE:
305-451-2353

FAX:
305-451-4789

ADDRESS:
Jules' Undersea Lodge
51 Shoreland Dr.
Key Largo, Florida 33037

SERVICES: Couples renting the entire lodge for the night will receive flowers, music, and a caviar appetizer. Special occasions such as birthdays and anniversaries can be accommodated with extras such as cakes, flowers, or special food. Just call ahead to plan for these additions.

DINING: Couples renting the entire lodge will receive a gourmet breakfast and dinner prepared by the lodge's "mer-chef", as well as snacks and drinks in the small kitchen.

RATES: The lodge is $1,050.00 per night for couples. If you're willing to share the lodge, you can get packages for $250.00 to $350.00 per person per night.

Runaway Hill Club

Harbour Island, Bahamas

Harbour Island, Bahamas is home to one of the most relaxing and comfortable retreats available, Runaway Hill Club. With

the warm, tropical breezes blowing off the Atlantic Ocean, guests cannot help but to sit back, relax and soak in the tropical atmosphere. The local residents are ready to welcome visitors with open arms. A friendly and fun loving people, they make guests feel right at home.

Rooms are decorated to project the feel of home as well. Large, light, airy and colorful, the rooms are air-conditioned and equipped with ceiling fans and private baths.

Working on a tan has never been easier. Lying on the pink sand beach or taking a refreshing swim in the ocean is a relaxing way to spend a day. Snorkeling and diving are other options that allow guests to enjoy all this island setting has to offer. Shopping and restaurants are located nearby and offer an array of items and foods sold by local merchants.

Wonderful meals are served at breakfast and lunch on the veranda, with a gourmet dinner served in style in the dining room. After dinner, taking a slow, leisurely stroll along the beach has never been more romantic.

For those that desire a relaxed, romantic, and tropical getaway retreat, Runaway Hill Club is a great choice!

Runaway Hill Club

CONTACT:

WEBSITE:
www.runawayhill.com

PHONE:
800-728-9803 or 242-333-2150

FAX:
242-333-2420

ADDRESS:
Runaway Hill Club
P.O. Box EL 27031
Harbour Island, Bahamas

SERVICES: Swimming from the beach, diving, snorkeling, and enjoying the sun are main activities at Runaway Hill Club. Shopping and restaurant alternatives are located nearby.

DINING: Breakfast and lunch are served daily on the veranda. Gourmet dinners are eloquently served in the dining room. A few local restaurants provide other dining options.

RATES: Seasonal rates range from $210.00 to $260.00 per night. All guests must be 16 years of age or older. Call for details.

Paradise Stream - Caesars Pocono Resorts

Mt. Pocono, Pennsylvania

Famous for years as a lover's getaway, the Pocono Mountains is the setting for Paradise Stream, a member of the Caesars Pocono Resorts. This is the playground couples have flocked to . . . and left with a renewed sense of fun and romance.

Paradise Stream has four of the most romantic and unforgettable suites available. Each is equipped with a cozy fireplace, king size bed, color television, VCR, and refrigerator. Some of the rooms offer a heart shaped whirlpool, heart shaped pool, private pool, private sauna, steam shower for two, Bose wave radio, massage table, and whirlpool bath for two. One suite even offers the resort's famous seven-foot champagne glass whirlpool, an exciting experience for any couple.

Activities outside the suites provide for romantic nature walks, swimming, archery, fishing, rowboats, paddle boats, tennis, miniature golf, and bicycling. The spa facility has a host of activities including racquetball and a heated pool. There is also the Parrot Lounge or Jungle Café where guests can enjoy a refreshing drink or snack.

Breakfast can be enjoyed in bed or in the Huntress Dining Room. Their wide array of breakfast items will ensure no guest goes away hungry. Dinner begins with complimentary hors d'oeuvres, then it's the enticing smells and tastes of exquisite cuisine prepared by Paradise Stream's first class chefs. After dinner, spend the night dancing to melodious sounds or laughing at the talent in the comedy club.

If you're a racecar buff, you'll love the Pocono Raceway weekend getaway. This weekend includes a trip to an official NASCAR sanctioned 2.5-mile super speedway where you'll have the opportunity to drive a real 800 horsepower Winston Cup style racecar. A professional instructor will be on hand to help with all the basics.

Caesars is also host to many other theme specialty getaways throughout the year including a spring and fall golf tournament; a special Roman weekend with old time festivities and live entertainment is brought in for the Oldies and Juke Box Hero's Weekends.

Paradise Stream is only one of Caesars Pocono Resorts locations. Cove Haven, Pocono Palace, and Brookdale resorts are all located nearby and are as equally impressive as their sister resort Paradise Stream. Let the romance of the beautiful and majestic Pocono Mountains fill your heart and soul on your next romantic adventure!

Paradise Stream

CONTACT:

WEBSITE:
www.caesarspoconoresorts.com

EMAIL:
cpr@starwoodhotels.com

PHONE:
877-822-3333 (If driving in)
877-822-4444
(For all-inclusive with airfare)
570-839-8881 (Direct line)

FAX:
570-839-1842

ADDRESS:
Paradise Stream
Route 940
Mount Pocono, Pennsylvania 18344

SERVICES: Mountain lake setting allows for nature walks, paddle boating, hiking, and fishing. Other activities include tennis, miniature golf, swimming, and spa facilities with racquetball and heated pool. Some in-room amenities allow for whirlpool baths for two and private swimming.

DINING: Breakfast may be served either in room, in bed, or enjoyed in the Huntress Dining Room. Hors d'oeuvres are served prior to the evening meal. Dinners are prepared by professional chefs and offer an array of cuisine.

RATES: Four suites are available at Paradise Stream. Specials are offered and rates can be obtained through an online form, email, or phone.

Swept Away Negril

Negril, Jamaica

Swept Away is an all-inclusive resort set right on the spectacular, seven-mile beach at Negril in Jamaica. Here you will stay in a lush garden setting with beautiful palm trees and exotic, tropical plants. Within this garden setting, are several low-slung

white buildings with red roofs housing spacious suites with large verandahs. Your suite is equipped with comfortable furnishings, air conditioners, lovely tile floors, and wooden shutters allowing you to let in the Caribbean sun as much or as little as you like.

You might be tempted to stay in your room, but you'll inevitably be coaxed out by the sound of the surf just yards away. Don't bother putting your shoes on. Your walk to the beach is a short one at Swept Away. Lay on a lounge chair listening to the comforting sounds of the waves or get into the action with one of several water sport possibilities. Snorkel, scuba, windsurf, or take a ride on a glass bottom boat to view the fantastic array of aquatic life in the area.

When you've had enough of the beach, play a round of complimentary golf, visit the sports complex, or opt for a spa treatment. Treatments at the spa are fee based, but you'll come away feeling pampered and refreshed.

A continental breakfast is available on your private verandah for a leisurely start to your day. There are five restaurants available onsite for your daily meals featuring everything from gourmet cuisine, to vegetarian specialties, and simple grilled sandwiches. Additionally, the property's four bars will keep your thirst continually quenched with their famed fruit concoctions and frozen specialties.

When the sun goes down, the party at Swept Away is just heating up. Take in the nightly show, or dance to the reggae sounds on the dance floor. Reggae dance classes are available during the day to get you ready to show off some new moves. With so much to do at the resort, you may not find time to venture out, but if you do, you'll discover that the area around Negril has much to offer as well. Ask your hosts about available tours, shopping, horseback riding, parasailing and more.

Swept Away Negril

CONTACT:

WEBSITE:
www.sweptaway.com

EMAIL:
info@couples.com

PHONE:
800-268-7537 or 305-668-0008

ADDRESS:
Swept Away Negril
7775 NW 48th Street, Suite 150
Miami, Florida 33166

SERVICES: Services at all-inclusive Swept Away are extensive and include all meals, snacks, beverages, wine and cocktails, activities, water sports, scuba diving, golf green fees at nearby courses, catamaran cruise, select off-site excursions, airport transfers, taxes and gratuities. Other services, such as massage, are available for a fee.

DINING: Five restaurants are available for your all-inclusive dining including a main restaurant, a gourmet restaurant, a veggie bar serving vegetarian meals, and two casual beach side eateries. Four onsite bars offer daily fresh fruit blends and frozen delights along with a variety of first-rate liquors. Breakfasts are normally served on your private verandah.

RATES: Swept Away requires a three night minimum stay. Rates per couple for a three night stay range from $1650.00 to $2250.00 depending on your accommodations and the time of year.

Resorts

Club Med Val Thorens Freestyle

France

When planning the ultimate, all-inclusive, adult vacation destination Club Med includes just about everything imaginable! With five adult village locations, the hardest decision you will have to make is where you would like to go. Club Med Val Thorens Freestyle offers a different type of resort. For those that do not wish the warmth of the tropics, this resort will fit your desire for cooler temperatures.

Located in the beautiful setting of the French Alps, Val Thorens Freestyle provides plenty of entertainment for the skiing enthusiast. Snowboarding and ice skating also makes this resort a true winter lover's paradise. After a vigorous day on the slopes you can sit back and relax in the sauna to warm up. Or guests may wish to take a refreshing dip in the large heated swimming pool. If more activity is desired, try a work out in the fitness center.

Val Thorens Freestyle has one restaurant for a relaxing and intimate dinner for two. After dinner, guests can enjoy the spectacular beauty of the French Alps while sipping their favorite beverage at the bar, or enjoy the Club Med evening entertainment.

There are 180 rooms at Val Thorens Freestyle each with its own shower room, hairdryer, telephone, TV and personal safe. The resort is seasonal and is open from the end of November through the beginning of May.

Try something different for your next romantic getaway. Call and reserve your stay at Val Thorens Freestyle! If a mountain resort is not the desired destination location, then try one of the other four Club Med adult villages. Each has its own unique set of amenities, but all offer the same quality and service that is Club Med!

SERVICES: Guests may enjoy skiing, snowboarding, swimming pool, sauna, nightclub activities, tennis, squash and fitness center. Ski lifts are available and slopes offer a variety of skill levels.

DINING: One restaurant is available for wonderfully prepared meals. One bar provides spirits and other beverages.

RATES: 180 rooms are available with rates starting at $500.00. The prices include accommodations, all meals, unlimited wine, beer and soft drinks with lunch and dinner, sports equipment (excluding snow skiing and snowboarding equipment), sports instruction and nightly entertainment. Call for details. Information can also be requested online.

Club Med Val Thorens Freestyle

CONTACT:

WEBSITE:
www.clubmed.com

EMAIL:
online request form

PHONE:
888-WEB-CLUB (932-2582)
04-79-00-04-83

FAX:
04-79-01-15-19

ADDRESS:
Club Med Val Thorens Freestyle
73440 Saint Martin de Belleville
France

LaSOURCE

St. George's, Grenada, West Indies

LaSOURCE is the only all-inclusive resort on the lovely south Caribbean Island of Grenada. It was created to be an ideal

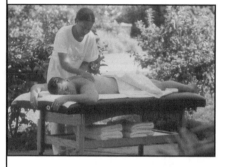

escape for hurried executives and other stressed adults. Here, the goal is relaxation of the body and renewal of the mind. An abundance of sun, sand, and sea, along with an extensive list of relaxing and rejuvenating activities, allows LaSOURCE to accomplish this worthy goal with great success.

Your stay at LaSOURCE will be one of luxurious comfort. All rooms at the resort have romantic four-poster beds, elegant marble floors, and a private bath and shower. You'll also enjoy amenities such as telephones, clock radios, a mini refrigerator, and hair dryer. All rooms face the ocean and have either a bal-

cony or terrace. Many of the second floor rooms have dramatic cathedral ceilings, as well.

Sports enthusiasts will marvel at the variety of activities included in the room price such as tennis, volleyball, archery, golf, and fencing. For water lovers, LaSOURCE offers sailing, scuba, snorkeling, water aerobics, and two fresh water swimming pools. Keep fit while on vacation in LaSOURCE's well-equipped gym. Use the equipment alone or join others for a class of stretching, toning, aerobics, or power walking. Interested in strengthening the body and calming the mind all at the same time? LaSOURCE provides classes in Tai Chi, Yoga, and meditation, all designed to help you relieve stress and gain inner balance.

For an afternoon of exquisite pampering, head to The Oasis, the resort's very own spa facility. Choose from any of the many complimentary services such as massage, aromatherapy, seaweed wrap, reflexology, and other treatments that will leave you tranquil and refreshed.

In between all this pampering and activity, you're sure to get hungry. LaSOURCE's great house restaurant offers a daily breakfast buffet and an a la carte dinner menu and the more casual, poolside terrace restaurant offers a daily lunch buffet. The terrace bar is open daily as a relaxing gathering place with board games and tennis tables. For evening entertainment, visit the piano bar and sing along to soothing melodies. At the beach, you'll be given a flag to plant in the sand when you're ready for your next cooling drink as you soak in the sun and surf.

SERVICES: LaSOURCE offers an extensive list of activities on land and sea including sports, spa treatments, gym equipment, fitness classes, and scuba lessons.

DINING: A breakfast buffet and a la carte dinner are served daily in the house restaurant onsite. For lunch, sample the buffet offered at the poolside terrace restaurant. Meal prices are included in your daily room rate.

RATES: Rates are from $400.00 to $900.00 per room per night based on double occupancy. Rates vary according to room accommodations and time of year.

Resorts

Caribbean Reef Club

Puerto Morales, Mexico

The Caribbean Reef Club is a couples-only, clothing optional resort in Puerto Morales, Mexico, just a twenty-minute drive from the bustling resort town of Cancun. The Caribbean Reef Club is smaller than some resorts in the area with just 40 rooms, but has plenty of amenities for its guests and offers a more intimate atmosphere. There is a large freshwater swimming pool, jacuzzi, non-motorized water sports, volleyball, and after dinner dancing.

The club has a very relaxed attitude and it's a good place to try going nude for the first time. Nudity is not mandatory at any time. This will offer you an excellent chance to try something new at your own pace. Rest assured, a variety of people in all shapes and sizes as well as all ages, come to Caribbean Reef Club to enjoy their time in the sun without the restrictions of clothing. The friendly unobtrusive atmosphere will have you freely strolling about unhampered in no time. The beach areas, pool, and jacuzzi are all open to nudity, but because

Mexican beaches are all considered public, you'll have to have swim trunks or bikini bottoms as you get closer to the water. Women are always allowed to go topless. Clothing is required in the dining area, the main bar, bar deck, and informal dining room.

Cuisine at the club features American and Mexican favorites with an infusion of fresh seafood and luscious tropical fruit. There are also plenty of light and healthy options for anyone wishing to watch their diet while on vacation. You'll also have a variety of cocktails and tropical thirst quenchers available at the bar.

Don your clothes and spend the day sightseeing in this magical part of Mexico. You can go on snorkeling and scuba diving expeditions, shop at one of the many stores in Cancun, take a fishing trip, or visit the fabulous Mayan ruins at Chitzen Itza. In

the evening, gather at the plaza in Puerto Plata to interact with natives, or drive to Cancun for international restaurants and an active nightlife. However, you never have to leave the Caribbean Reef Club for anything, as dancing and dining are right here.

SERVICES: All non-motorized water sports are included in the price of your stay including sail boating, ocean kayaking, and snorkeling off

the beach. You can also arrange fishing or scuba diving expeditions for an additional charge.

DINING: All meals are included in the price of your room. Breakfast and lunch are served in an open-air deck or in the informal dining area. Dinner is usually served in the Party Palapa. Special diets can be accommodated and the cuisine tends to feature Mexican and American favorites as well as plenty of seafood and tropical fruit.

RATES: Rates per night per couple are from $260.00 to $400.00 depending on accommodations and time of year. The resort is for adult couples only.

Caribbean Reef Club

CONTACT:

WEBSITE:
www.caribbeanreefclub.com

EMAIL:
info@caribbeanreefclub.com

PHONE:
888-5-CANCUN (888-522-6286)
or 800-3-CANCUN (800-322-6286)
(toll free in U.S. & Canada)
Outside the US call: 714-964-8453

FAX:
714-964-8453

ADDRESS:
Caribbean Reef Club
Puerto Morales, Mexico

Natadola Beach Resort

Natadola, Fiji Islands

Feel like one of the natives at this tropical paradise resort. Natadola Beach Resort, located in the exotic Fiji Islands, is the vacation retreat you will never forget.

Guests become one with the natives of the local village and can experience their unique lifestyles and customs. The people of Fiji are friendly and welcome visitors into their tropical island community.

Guest suites are roomy and colorfully decorated, reflecting the flavor of the local atmosphere. Each suite is equipped with a refrigerator, coffee/tea facilities, king or queen size bed, bottled water, and a comforting bathrobe. Guests may enjoy their own private garden courtyard and the swimming pool is only a few steps away from the door. There are 11 suites providing accommodations for up to 22 guests. This limit ensures guests top quality accommodations and service. Just think, no waiting for room in the swimming pool or for your waitress to serve you.

If you are looking for something to do, take a walk on the white sand beach and collect shells. Dive into the ocean or swimming pool.

Resorts

27

Check out what the underwater wildlife is up to while snorkeling or gallop across the beach on horseback. For the sports enthusiast, golf, tennis, or scuba diving can be arranged locally. How about trying out a boogie board?

After your day of adventure, try a meal of local favorites exquisitely prepared and lavishly presented. You may have your choice of dining areas. Maybe you would like to take your meal poolside. How about eating inside or sitting beachside under a wonderful sky while the waves lap the shore?

Natadola Beach Resort can also help in planning that special wedding, made even more special by the surroundings of the beautiful Fiji Islands.

SERVICES: Garden environment with swimming pool located immediately outside of suites. Activities available include boogie boarding, horseback riding, beach walking, snorkeling and sunbathing. Sport fishing, golf, tennis, and scuba diving arrangements can be made nearby.

DINING: Delicious meals are prepared from the freshest local ingredients and are served inside, poolside, or on the beach for your full enjoyment.

RATES: 11 suites are available. Rates vary and specials are often offered. Call or email for details.

Natadola Beach Resort

CONTACT:

WEBSITE:
www.natadola.com

EMAIL:
natadola@is.com.fj

PHONE:
679-721001
888-345-4669 (U.S. Only)
or 805-685-3555

FAX:
679-721000 or 805-685-3385 (U.S.)

ADDRESS:
Natadola Beach Resort
PMB 0381
Nadi Airport, Fiji Islands

Resorts

Palace Resorts - Aventura Palace

Carretera Cancun - Chetumal

Tropical delights await you just a mere 60 minutes from Cancun. Aventura Palace Rivera Maya in Carretera Cancun Chetumal is an adult only oasis that must be experienced.

This resort is an all–inclusive vacation destination that offers something for everyone! There are 85 acres of lush tropical gardens surrounding the resort. Their 1266 rooms offer only the best in amenities including individual climate control, satellite television, hair dryers, bathrobes, ceiling fans, in-room liquor dispensers, a fully stocked mini bar, purified water, coffee maker, in-room safe and a lavish décor. A variety of cheeses and sparkling wine will also be awaiting your arrival.

All meals and snacks are included. Dining facilities include cuisine with international and Mexican flavor. If spirits are your desire, there is a lobby bar, poolside bar and billiard room bar. The resort offers car rentals, a beauty salon, tobacco shop, 24-hour medical care and massages.

Aventura Palace also offers several wedding packages to help make your special day something to remember. A favorite spot for couples to tie the knot is in the gazebo overlooking the ocean. Just think, the wedding ceremony, reception and honeymoon all in one magnificent location!

Tours are available to wonderfully romantic destinations. Visit the historical ruins and pyramids at Chitzen Itza or Coba. World famous Chitzen Itza also offers a tour with a wondrous display of light and sound.

If touring is not your favorite pastime, then how about swimming in a large indoor or outdoor pool? Try out a diving tank, play beach volleyball, take a relaxing sauna, dancing, bicycling, a vigorous workout in a full gym, tennis or just sitting back and soaking up the sun. There are also three full gyms, a ten foot climbing tower, an obstacle course, an ocean front yoga hut, an aerobic room and full service spa. There are also nightly theme parties! What more could you want in a vacation? Aventura Palace is a true vacation palace and paradise!

SERVICES: There are many activities and services available at Aventura Palace, which include but are not limited to, massages, car rentals, beauty salon, 24-hour medical services, indoor pool, outdoor pool, nightly theme parties, full gym, beach volley-ball, salon games, dancing, cooking and cocktail lessons, badminton, and tours to local attractions.

DINING: All meals and imported or domestic beverages are included and can be found at several locations within the resort. Food varieties offered include Mexican and international cuisine.

RATES: Rates for the 1,266 rooms are seasonal and depend on the type of room and number of persons in your party. See their website for more information, request a brochure, or make reservations.

Resorts

Bedarra Island

Bedarra Island, Australia

Bedarra is a breathtakingly beautiful island of rainforest wilderness off Australia's tropical north coast. The resort is designed to be a private and romantic escape for adults who desire absolute tranquility. On the island, you'll stay in one of 15 villas surrounded by lush rainforest. The villas are available in three different styles—two story, split-level, and premium. Each of these luxury accommodations comes with a king size bed, TV and VCR, stocked mini bar, CD-stereo system, large bathroom, private balconies, an aromatherapy oil burner, bath robes, air-conditioning and much more. Most of the villas also offer fabulous views of the Pacific Ocean as well as your own private hammock to take an afternoon nap while listening to the waves break on the beach nearby.

You're free to spend days at your own pace on Bedarra Island, so lounge by the saltwater pool all day if you like or choose to explore the island. Beach picnics are a favorite with guests and there are several private beaches around the island. They are perfect for a romantic rendezvous. Other complimentary activities guests can enjoy include tennis, fishing, snorkeling, use of the resort's catamarans, sailboards and paddle skids. You can also use a motorized dinghy to scoot around the island's shores and explore neighboring islands as well. For an additional fee, you can join scheduled snorkeling and scuba diving trips to the renowned Great Barrier Reef, or tour nearby Dunk Island for golf, water-skiing, parasailing, horseback riding and more

Three meals are served daily at Bedarra Island featuring gourmet touches and an emphasis on fresh seafood. There's also a bar for relaxing serving several highly rated Australian wines, beers and a variety of other spirits. Import beers are also available. The bar is open 24-hours a day. The resort also offers a variety of massage therapies from Reiki to complete body massage to help you relax.

Bedarra Island

CONTACT:

WEBSITE:
www.poresorts.com

EMAIL:
resorts_reservations@poaustralia.com

PHONE:
07-4068-8233 or 800-225-9849

FAX:
07-4068-8215

ADDRESS:
P.O. Box 268
Mission Beach, QLD 4852
Austrailia

SERVICES: Bedarra Island gives its guests access to videos, books, games, and a CD library. There is also a postal service, laundry service, safety deposit box availability, and Internet access in the lobby. Guests enjoy complementary snorkeling, fishing, catamarans, motorized dinghies, and gourmet picnic lunches. Massage, snorkeling tours to the Great Barrier Reef, and a variety of activities on Dunk Island are available for an additional fee.

DINING: The resort has an open-air restaurant serving breakfast, lunch and dinner a la carte. There is also a 24-hour lounge bar on the property. All meals and beverages are included in the price of your stay. For those seeking something a little more romantic, gourmet picnic baskets are available for beach side outings upon request.

RATES: Room rates per person, per night are from $840.00 to $950.00 AUD ($420.00 to $475.00 USD) based on double occupancy and $1040.00 to $1150.00 AUD ($520.00 to $575.00 USD) based on single occupancy. Bedarra Island is designed for adults only.

Resorts

Salish Lodge & Spa

Snoqualmie, Washington

If you are looking for that romantic setting that is different than the normal island getaway, then try Salish Lodge & Spa.

Located in the great Pacific Northwest and nestled in the majestic Snoqualmie Falls, Salish Lodge offers its guests the best in accommodations and atmosphere. 91 deluxe guest rooms and suites are cozy and charming. Each has a whirlpool tub and wood fireplace. Couples can get even cozier wrapped up in the down filled comforter and sunken into the luxurious feather bed. All rooms are also equipped with robes, coffee and coffee makers, iron and ironing board, and hair dryer.

Spending the day touring local towns allows for shopping, museum adventures, and exploration of the local wineries, breweries, gardens, and parks. With Seattle only 30 miles away, a day trip would be an ace in the perfect hand of your vacation. The spa facilities offer an enticing array of decadent services to pamper your partner, yourself, or both.

Guests may start their day with the Salish Lodge's infamous five-course breakfast. Then, if they can even think about eating again, lunch and dinner are also provided. The Dining Room serves elaborate gourmet cuisine, such as roasted venison, smoked salmon and braised veal, and sports an award winning wine list. For those desiring a lighter meal, breakfast and lunch are served in The Attic. Dinner can also be enjoyed in The Attic on weekends and during holidays.

Full wedding packages are also offered for those getting married. The helpful staff can assist you in making all the arrangements and host your wedding in one of its five ballrooms.

Although Salish Lodge & Spa does accept children, activities are geared toward adult interests and special packages are often offered just for adults.

Your next vacation could be in the beauty of the Snoqualmie Falls. Stay at Salish Lodge & Spa and treat yourself to a peaceful, calming, cozy, and romantic vacation.

SERVICES: In-room whirlpool tubs and local tours allow for some entertainment. Shopping, museums, garden walks and a theater are all located within 30 miles of the lodge. The resort also has a fitness center, sauna, steam room, as well as a variety of spa services to help you relax.

DINING: Elegant meals are served daily in either of the two restaurants overlooking the valley and rolling hills. The Dining Room offers a famous and elaborate five-course breakfast, and offers a vast selection of local wines for dinner. The Attic serves food throughout the entire day and offers guests a more casual dining experience. Local restaurants are available for an optional alternative.

RATES: Rates are $229.00 to $419.00 per night with specials often offered. Call for details.

The Caves Resort

Negril, Jamaica

This unique resort sits on volcanic rock formations on the Jamaican coast near Negril. The resort is small and intimate, offering only ten thatched-roof huts for its guests. A variety of amenities are available depending on the accommodations you choose. The smallest and most basic huts are comfortable for two and feature romantic, mosquito netted beds, sitting areas, and an outside shower. On the other end of the spectrum is the two-story, two-bedroom Sun Dancer suite offering a traditional bath and shower, living area, and kitchenette. Most have ocean views and all are just a short walk to the rocky coastline.

While The Caves Resort does not have direct access to beaches, its unique location on the volcanic rock offers a very distinctive experience for swimmers and snorkelers. Lovely rock stairways and convenient ladders lead swimmers down to the water where intriguing caves are waiting to be discovered.

Don complimentary snorkeling gear and take a look at the reef that flanks the property where an abundance of both sea life and fascinating natural formations await. The truly adventurous can dive off the cliffs into the 30-foot water or jump through a blowhole in the rock for an unforgettable experience.

The property itself offers a saltwater pool, sunning deck, sauna, and spa facilities. Use the complimentary bicycles to explore the two-acre property on land or opt to spend a day off the property. One of the best beaches in Jamaica is just a ten-minute drive from The Caves. Your hosts will be happy to tell you how to get there as well as inform you about other tours and activities available in the area on land and sea.

The Caves Resort

CONTACT:

WEBSITE:
www.thecavesresort.com

EMAIL:
reservations@islandoutpost.com
thecaves@islandoutpost.com

PHONE:
876-957-0270
or 305-531-8800 (Reservations)

FAX:
876-957-4930

ADDRESS:
The Caves Resort
Negril, Jamaica

SERVICES: Day tours and land and water sport excursions can be arranged through the front desk for an additional fee.

DINING: All-inclusive dining is available in The Caves' breezy, gazebo-styled dining room. Enjoy breakfast, lunch, and dinner all embodied with tastes and textures from authentic Jamaican cuisine.

RATES: Rates per room per night are from $425.00 to $875.00 depending on your accommodations. Room rates are based on single or double occupancy. Rent the entire property for a night and 24 guests can stay for $5,143.00 or about $215.00 per guest. Guests must be 16 years old or older.

Resorts

Yasawa Island Resort

Yasawa Island, Fiji

At this small island resort, the philosophy is that you should be able to do what you want to do, when you want to do it. Hinging off this way of thinking, Yasawa Island Resort has been designed to be private and unhurried with a wide variety of activities available on your timetable. After flying over the spectacular blue and green water to arrive on the island, you'll be taken to your private bure to get acquainted with your accommodations.

The property has only 16 one and two bedroom bures set amid dense tropical surroundings to ensure your privacy. Your bure will provide you with a king sized bed, private bath, telephone, CD radio, coffee maker, refrigerator, iron with ironing board, personal safe, and hair dryer. For your comfort, each room also has ceiling fans and an air conditioner, just in case the ocean breezes aren't enough to keep you cool. Outside you'll find a private sunbathing deck, which serves as an excellent location for secluded relaxation.

During the day, be sure to head to the beach and enjoy the sun, sand, and incredible waters. On the beach, you'll find complimentary kayaks, paddleboats, and catamarans. There are also many private beaches all around the island suitable for some romantic fun or a pre-arranged private picnic. If you can pull yourself away from the water, consider a hike up through the hills and rainforest. The vegetation here is truly spectacular. Tours of the local villages, as well as scuba excursions and fishing trips are also available for an additional fee.

Dining is an important part of your experience at Yasawa Island Resort and your hosts will make sure it's also a memorable one. Cuisine features Asian and European specialties created around the area's abundance of fresh seafood and unique

Resorts

produce. In addition, the resort claims to have one of the finest wine lists in Fiji, featuring wine selections from Australia and New Zealand and champagne from France.

If you're vacationing at Yasawa Island Resort for a special occasion such as a wedding, honeymoon, anniversary, or birthday, don't hesitate to ask for special arrangements from your hosts. They are happy to work with guests to create memories of such happy occasions that will last forever. Typically, the staff requires 48 hours notice for special arrangements.

Yasawa Island Resort

CONTACT:

WEBSITE:
www.yasawa.com

EMAIL:
yasawa@connect.com.fj

PHONE:
679-672-2266

FAX:
679-672-4456

ADDRESS:
Yasawa Island Resort
P.O. Box 10128
Nadi Airport, Fiji Islands

SERVICES: Many activities are included in the price of your stay including tennis, croquet, snorkeling, kayaking, and many others. Village trips are also available.

DINING: All meals are included and feature a mixture of European and Asian cuisine with an emphasis on fresh seafood and produce. Wine and champagne are available for an additional fee.

RATES: Room rates per night range from $820.00 to $1275.00 based on double occupancy and include all meals, non-alcoholic beverages, and all activities excluding scuba diving, game fishing, and spa treatments.

Pleasure Cove Lodge

Stann Creek District, Belize

There are tropical resorts and then there is Pleasure Cove Lodge. Located in the Stann Creek District of Belize, this adult only resort offers a private and peaceful atmosphere with the utmost in personalized service.

Five guest rooms and one suite are the available accommodations. Guest rooms have an earthy décor and provide guests with a queen size bed, or two double beds, private bath enhanced by its glass wall shower, and air conditioning. The suite is your tropical home, offering a living room and kitchenette among other amenities. The suite also allows its guests to enjoy a private patio.

Spend a romantic day exploring the jungle or caves, snorkeling around the impressively beautiful coral reefs, diving in crystal clear turquoise waters, or being mystified by the ancient Mayan ruins.

Before a day of adventure begins, breakfast will fuel the body with a wide array of items that include fresh juice, eggs, and fresh baked breads. Lunches include a lighter choice of salads, sandwiches and daily specials. Guests may top off their exciting day with enticing dinners that start with a salad or soup, continue to a vast variety of entrees, and

CONTACT:

WEBSITE:
www.pleasurecovelodge.com

EMAIL:
vacations@pleasurecovelodge.com

PHONE:
011- 501-520-7089

ADDRESS:
Pleasure Cove Lodge
Sitee Point, Hopkins Village
Stann Creek District, Belize

finishes up with an elaborate and sin-fully delicious offering of desserts.

Enchanting! Private! Romantic! Everything a couple could want in a vacation, and Pleasure Cove Lodge has it all. With its tropical Caribbean setting, it is truly a paradise lover's hot spot!

SERVICES: Activities included are swimming, snorkeling, jungle exploration, and beach walks. Tour packages are offered for diving, fishing, touring the Mayan ruins, and cave explorations.

DINING: Elaborate breakfasts of juice, breads, eggs, and other items start the day. Lunch choices include sand-wiches, salads, burritos, and daily specials. Evening meals offer soups and salads, an exquisitely prepared array of main courses, and delicious desserts. Pleasure Cove Lodge also offers coffees and many other drink favorites. Meals are included in some packages.

RATES: There are five guest rooms and one suite available for accommodating adults only. Rates are seasonal and range from $90.00 to $320.00 per night, with special packages offered. Call or email for details.

Resorts

Rendezvous

Located in the elegant tropics of the West Indies and catering to adult couples, Rendezvous is the perfect all-inclusive setting for a romantic vacation, honeymoon, or anniversary celebration.

With palms swaying overhead and the crash of the sea, Rendezvous offers its guests an exquisitely beautiful atmosphere and a vacation that includes it all. 100 rooms and suites await their guests. Decorated in a Caribbean flavor and equipped with everything from a king size bed to an in-room safe, these rooms are your

home away from home. Each room also has a balcony or terrace and an ocean view.

Couples will enjoy spending time together swimming in one of the two fresh water pools or relaxing in the sauna. A romantic time at play is never out of the question with two tennis courts and a golf practice area available. Water sport activities are numerous at this beachside resort. Kayaking, windsailing, snorkeling, and local scuba diving are available.

A variety of restaurants provide the luxury of different dining styles and tastes. The Terrace Restaurant offers a buffet style offering, allowing guests to eat 'til their hearts are content. The Trysting Place has guests in the romantic setting of a fine dining

CONTACT:

WEBSITE:
www.rendezvous.com.lc

EMAIL:
reservations@theromanticholiday.com

PHONE:
800-544-2883

FAX:
781-821-1568

ADDRESS:
Rendezvous
Malabar Beach
P.O. Box 190
Castries, St. Lucia, West Indies

restaurant. Couples can luxuriate over the a la carte menu with many gourmet treats.

Romance can be found every night at Rendezvous. The nightlife offers couples a chance to kick back and listen to the tinkling sounds of the ivories at the piano bar or join in a sing-a-long. Karaoke is another form of enjoyment and fun. Dancing the night away will light the sparks in any relationship. Music flows as free and easy as the drinks at the bar.

Imagine a wedding with the background of the sea, stenciled with palm and ocean birds in flight. At Rendezvous, it can happen. The best part is, you are already at your honeymoon destination. Make Rendezvous the choice for your next romantic vacation for two. The islands are waiting!

SERVICES: Guests can find two pools, two tennis courts, massages, gym, book exchange, archery range, golf practice area, water sports, tours, nightly entertainment, three bars with beach service, scuba excursions, and bicycling tours.

DINING: Meals are provided and offer guests a choice in dining facilities and styles. Buffet meals are served at The Terrace Restaurant, while The Trysting Place offers fine dining in a romantic setting.

RATES: Rates vary, call or email for details.

Resorts

The Occidental Royal Hideaway Playacar

Playa del Carmen, Mexico

This all-inclusive adult only resort sits right on the beautiful beach of the Yucatan Peninsula overlooking the turquoise waters of the Caribbean Sea. The large resort is styled to reflect Spanish colonial architecture. It is made up of eleven two and three story buildings on 13 acres of lush tropical gardens with winding rivers, fountains and numerous waterfalls that tie everything together.

The resort hosts 178 lavish guestrooms and offers guests four-room types, including two presidential suites. A fresh fruit basket will be in your room waiting your arrival. Each room has its own private terrace or balcony with a spectacular view of the ocean or the plush resort gardens. All the rooms have air-conditioning, a ceiling fan, marbled bathroom amenities, robes, slippers, satellite television with VCR, stereo with CD player, selection of personal toiletries, hydromassage jet tubs, a safety deposit box and a refreshment bar.

The high vaulted ceilings and elaborate chandeliers in most of the restaurants and common areas give you the feeling of royalty as you wander around the resort. You will have no trouble finding something to keep you occupied during your stay. A full day schedule of activities starts bright and early every morning and runs until about 4:30 p.m. Some of the activities include tennis, pool volleyball, bingo, sight seeing bike tours, towel sculpture, Spanish lessons, darts, horseshoes, bocce ball, dance lessons, cooking lessons, diving lessons and much more. Or for those who want to take things a little slower, the resort has three swimming pools and three smaller relaxation pools where you can kick your feet up and enjoy a cool beverage under the shade of a tall swaying palm tree.

Getting married? The Occidental Royal Hideaway Playacar offers a wide variety of wedding packages to make it a day to remember. They even throw in the cake, photos and bouquet for the bride.

The Occidental Royal Hideaway

CONTACT:

WEBSITE:
www.royalhideaways.com

EMAIL:
reservations@rhplacar.allegroresorts.com

PHONE:
800-999-9182 or 52-984-873-4500

ADDRESS:
The Occidental Royal Hideaway Playacar
Lote Hotelero #7 Fracc. Playacar
Playa del Carmen, Quintana Roo C.P. 77710 Mexico

SERVICES: All-inclusive services include a welcome bottle of champagne and cool towel upon arrival, tennis clinics, wine with dinner, 24-hour room service, daily poolside and beach activities, full fitness center with jacuzzi and nightly entertainment. There are a variety of non-motorized water sports available. You also have use of facilities at nearby sister properties.

DINING: All meals and beverages are included in the room price. The resort hosts five a la carte specialty restaurants, most with veranda seating for those who enjoy outdoor dining. There are also three bars on the premises including a cigar bar.

RATES: Room rates per person per night range from $355.00 to $1030.00 and varies according to room type and time of year. The Occidental Royal Hideaway Playacar does not allow anyone under 13 years of age and there is a maximum of 3 adults per room. Couples and singles are welcome.

The Terra Cotta Inn

Palm Springs, California

The Terra Cotta Inn is a tastefully done clothing optional resort in beautiful, sunny Palm Springs. As guests of the resort, you'll stay in a spacious room available with or without a full kitchen and decorated in the soothing colors of the southwest. Each room has a king size bed, separate seating area, refrigerator, microwave, coffee maker, cable TV, and VCR. Optional room amenities include private patios, sunken tubs, and private entrances.

Start your day with a walk through the garden-styled grounds on your way to a complimentary poolside breakfast with the

other guests. You can get started working on your all-over tan right away if you wish. At Terra Cotta, you're encouraged to do whatever is comfortable for you.

After breakfast, you can continue working on your tan, swim in the pool, go back to your room to relax, arrange to have a massage, or venture out to see the lovely Palm Springs area. Golfers will be in heaven here, as there are several world-class courses available. Your hosts can even arrange a tee-time for you if you like. Guests of the inn also enjoy access to a local tennis club sporting fabulous views of the surrounding mountains. Opportunities for shopping and dining in Palm Springs are top notch and your hosts can help you

CONTACT:

WEBSITE:
www.sunnyfun.com

EMAIL:
info@sunnyfun.com

PHONE:
800-SUNNYFUN (800-786-6938)
760-322-6059 (Palm Springs)

FAX:
760-322-4169

ADDRESS:
The Terra Cotta Inn
2388 E. Racquet Club Road
Palm Springs, California 92262-2629

with recommendations if you're having trouble deciding where to go. If you'd prefer to stay in for meals, take advantage of Terra Cotta's Restaurant Express. This service allows for meals delivered to your door from several participating restaurants.

SERVICES: Terra Cotta Inn offers a variety of spa services onsite for varying fees.

DINING: A continental style breakfast featuring Starbucks coffees is included in your room price. For an extra fee, you can request soups or salads for lunch from Terra Cotta's catering partner. Late afternoon snacks are also included in your stay. Dinner can be delivered to your room.

RATES: Deluxe rooms are $125.00 per night weekdays and $139.00 per night on weekends. Deluxe rooms with kitchens are $139.00 per night on weekdays and $159.00 per night on weekends. Ask about specials for multiple night stays during the week and for seven-day packages.

Resorts

Twelve Degrees North

St. George's, Grenada, West Indies

Twelve Degrees North is a small and quiet resort for couples desiring a calm setting without lots of people and action. With only eight units and on-site hosts, the property feels more residential than commercial. You'll have a maid and cook in your room each morning to clean and prepare both breakfast and dinner if you like. Meals are normally served on your private balcony. After breakfast, take a walk down to the property's private beach area for snorkeling or kayaking, or go for a swim in the freshwater pool. When you get thirsty, you'll discover that there is a bar area near the beach where you can mix your own drinks. If you'd like to simply lounge and read, the owners keep a supply of paperback books on hand for just this purpose. Hammocks are strung between palm trees poolside and are a favorite spot for guests to relax after an afternoon dip in the pool or stroll down the beach.

When you want to venture out from your hide-away at Twelve Degrees North, your hosts can help you pick an activity or tour around the island that's just right for you. Go on a fishing excursion or play a round of golf. You can also rent a car and simply explore. Grenada offers many shopping opportunities with great buys on locally made items. With a rich offering of restaurants in the area, you'll also want to try out some of the local cuisine, or find a spot that specializes in your favorite tastes. At night, you can either go back to your quiet room to turn in early and wake to the sunrise, or opt to party the night away at one of the island bars featuring jazz musicians or a steel drum band.

Grenada consists of three small islands totaling 133 square miles. Miles of picture perfect, sugar-fine white sandy beaches line each of the tropical mountainous islands. Some favorite tourist spots include the Sendall Tunnel, Fort George, the Botanical Gardens, or Leapers Hill.

Twelve Degrees North

CONTACT:

WEBSITE:
www.twelvedegreesnorth.com

EMAIL:
12degrsn@caribsurf.com

PHONE:
473-444-4580

ADDRESS:
Twelve Degrees North
P.O. Box 241
St. George's, Grenada, West Indies

SERVICES: At Twelve Degrees North, you'll have your own maid and cook daily, along with laundry service. You'll also be given floral arrangements and a bottle of rum punch for your room. The grounds offer a freshwater pool, tennis court and a private beach with easy access to snorkeling, rafts, kayaks and sunfish sailboats.

DINING: Each room is provided with a maid and a private cook who will prepare authentic gourmet meals for you each day. There are also stocked refrigerators in each room if you just wanted a late night snack. Numerous restaurants are nearby if you wanted to venture off-site for your meals.

RATES: In winter, one-bedroom apartments for two people are $225.00 per night and two-bedroom apartments for four people are from $350.00 per night. In summer, one-bedroom apartments for two people are $150.00 per night and two-bedroom apartments for four people are $265.00 per night. No children under 15 allowed.

Resorts

Sandals Dunn's River

Ocho Rios, Jamaica

Created for lovers, Sandals Resorts is a group of ten of the best all-inclusive resorts in the world. Located on four of the most exotic islands in the Caribbean, Sandals Resorts has it all! Offering a wide array of amenities, Sandals is the ultimate lover's paradise! From suites with a panoramic view of the sea to beautifully brilliant gardens, you are assured the best quality a resort can offer.

Sandals Dunn's River offers ultimate relaxation within the 256-room resort. Rooms include air conditioning, king size bed, hair dryer, phone, private bath, in-room safe, clock radio, satellite television, and coffeemaker.

Looking for romantic indulgences? Then maybe you will find it within one of the four restaurants at Sandals Dunn's River. Sandals Resorts offers the ultimate in gourmet dining experiences making them unlike any other all-inclusive resort. Is it a candlelit table for two for an intimate indoor dinner you are looking for? Sandals Resorts can provide that! Would you prefer spending that ultimately intimate dinner for two gazing at each other and at a magnificent moonlit seaside? Sandals can see to that too!

Maybe your interests lie below the sea! Sandals Dunn's River provides the highest quality scuba diving and water sports equipment and they back it with instructions from their staff of professionals. Their diving program is the Caribbean's most comprehensive all-inclusive program available. Nightlife can be found at any one of the seven bars located at Sandals Dunn's River. There are also nightly theme parties!

Sandals Dunn's River is an adult only retreat, as is their other resorts located in Jamaica, Antigua, St. Lucia and the Bahamas. It is the best of the best!

Treat yourself and your partner to the best vacation there is, a luxurious stay at Sandals Dunn's River. If this is not your choice, then one of the other nine locations is sure to fit your needs and desires.

Sandals Dunn's River is a golfer's paradise with the Sandals Golf & Country Club just minutes away. There is also a Pitch N' Putt golf course directly at the resort. You are welcome to play as often as you'd like and free transportation is provided to the country club. After a hard day on the fairway, relax with a massage. The resort is part of Sandals Signature Spa destinations featuring full and on-site European spa services for an extra fee.

Sandals Dunn's River

CONTACT:

WEBSITE:
www.sandals.com

EMAIL:
info@sandals.com

PHONE:
(888) SANDALS (726-3857)

ADDRESS:
Sandals Dunn's River
P.O. Box 51
Mamme Bay
Ocho Rios, Jamaica, W.I.

SERVICES: Swimming pool, scuba diving, water skiing, sailing, canoeing, snorkeling, complimentary golf, sauna, steam room, tropical gardens and four tennis courts are all available to guests of Sandals Dunn's River. Transportation to and from Sandals Golf & the Country club is also included.

DINING: Four restaurants offer a variety of dining favorites and styles. International, Italian, Caribbean and Western grill allow for a range of formal to casual dining experiences and cuisine. 24-hour a day room service is also provided for those who might want a late night snack.

RATES: Seasonal rates ranging from $245.00 to $470.00 per night with 256 rooms and suites available.

Resorts

Heather Lodge Resort

Minden, Ontario, Canada

Heather Lodge Resort is a cozy retreat for couples nestled in a beautiful woodland setting. With only 11 guest rooms, you can be sure that you'll get the pampering and individual attention you deserve from this intimate, family-run establishment. Each of the lodge's three available room sizes is equipped with a TV, bar refrigerator, and private bath. The largest rooms also have a fireplace and a private balcony with a view of the lake. No matter which room you choose to stay in, you'll find carefully chosen furniture and attention to decorating detail that makes your retreat both comfortable and romantic.

The main lodge is a friendly gathering place equipped with a billiard table, games table, and your choice of board games. Outside on the grounds, try your luck at shuffleboard or badminton. In the summer and fall months, venture on to the nearby trails to take in nature's ever changing beauty. You can also head to the lake for swimming, boating, and fishing adventures. Winter fun starts next door where you can rent snowmobiles for a wild and snowy ride through the forest. Any time of year, you can soothe the effects of an active day in the lodge's hot tub or sauna.

Meals at Heather Lodge Resort are as comforting and inviting as every other part of the experience here. Both breakfast and dinner is available to guests featuring North American cuisine infused with the flavors of the orient. Each night a choice of three entrees is offered, so you're sure to find a favorite every time.

SERVICES: Your hosts can direct you to a number of enjoyable excursions off site including golf, kayaking, and scenic flights over the area.

DINING: Heather Lodge offers breakfast and dinner to its guests each day in the dining room, or weather permitting, on the patio deck. Meals feature North American cuisine with an oriental accent for variety.

Heather Lodge Resort

CONTACT:

WEBSITE:
www.heatherlodge.com

EMAIL:
enquiry@heatherlodge.com

PHONE:
800-362-6676

ADDRESS:
Heather Lodge Resort
Minden, Ontario, Canada K0M 2K0

RATES: Call for exact prices. Rates vary according to season and longer stays may result in lower per night rates. Adults only. No pets.

Breezes Resorts

Nassau, Bahamas; Montego Bay & Runaway Bay, Jamaica

Tropics, tropics, and more tropics is what you will find when you arrive at any of these three Breezes Resorts that are for adults only, 16 years of age or older. Resorts located in Montego Bay & Runaway Bay, Jamaica and Nassau, Bahamas ensure a tropical paradise to be enjoyed and relished.

Breezes Bahamas is a luxurious super inclusive resort that is only rivaled by its sister resorts. Each of its 400 rooms is just waiting to thrill guests. Rooms are beautifully decorated and include coffee maker, CD player, in-room safe, iron, ironing board, satellite television, direct dial phone, hair dryer, and air conditioning.

Activities abound at all Breezes Resorts and Breezes Bahamas is no different. For the water lover, there is sailing, kayaking, swimming, water-skiing, scuba diving lessons, and windsurfing. Landlubbers will enjoy tennis, volleyball, bicycles, jogging trails, basketball, and golf, which require an additional fee. Sun worshiping can be found on the elegant white beaches or alongside any of the five pools. Jacuzzi and misting pools are also available. A fitness center keeps the physically inclined busy, while a game room will entertain the not so physically inclined.

Gambling can be found nearby on Cable Beach or Paradise Island. Many special activities are available including an all-weather, man made ice skating surface.

After a hard day of play, step into one of three restaurants located in Breezes Bahamas. From a pasta bar to buffet style dining, an excellent dinner awaits. The pool grill serves snacks during the afternoon and evening.

Ready to play some more? Okay, lets go to the disco and dance until 5am. Or, you could check out the live entertainment

Resorts

in the lobby bar. Breezes Bahamas also has theme nights that range from toga parties to afternoon tea.

Give Breezes Bahamas two days notice and they will provide the wedding furnishing a cake, license, marriage officer, witnesses, champagne and all paperwork.

Think Breezes Bahamas sounds wonderful, but really wanted to go to Jamaica? Then check out Breezes Montego Bay or Breezes Runaway Bay for many of the same features, amenities and offers. Breezes Resorts, where it's a breeze to plan your next vacation!

Breezes Resorts

CONTACT:

WEBSITE:
www.breezes.com

EMAIL:
info@superclubs.com

PHONE:
877-GO-SUPER (467-8737)

FAX:
954-925-0334

SERVICES: Pools, beaches, jacuzzi, swimming, water-skiing, kayaking, windsurfing, tours, basketball, tennis, shopping, fitness center, and other amenities too numerous to mention are provided by Breezes Resorts and all are included in the cost of your stay.

DINING: Buffet style meals, pasta bar, and snacks are offered in a wonderfully tropical atmosphere. All meals and drinks are included in your stay.

RATES: Rates vary depending on destination location. Call for details.

Blue Bay Resorts

Cancun & Puerto Vallarta, Mexico

Imagine lying on a beautiful, sandy beach soaking up a tropical sun, refreshed by a warm breeze blowing in from a radiant ocean! Sound good? Blue Bay Resorts has your place in the sun.

Blue Bay Resorts offer four different resorts for adults only, 16 years of age or older. Getaway Puerto Vallarta, Getaway Cancun, Club Puerto Vallarta, and Club Cancun are all-inclusive vacation destinations that offer everything a vacationing couple or single could want. At Blue Bay Getaway Cancun, the accommodations offer only the best in amenities, including satellite television, private bath with shower, air conditioning, direct dial telephones, a terrace or balcony, and an ocean view.

Delicious meals are included and can be enjoyed at any one of the four restaurants located at the resort. You can even enjoy a

nightly theme dinner. Snacks are also included. Sit back and have a relaxing drink in one of the three regular bars or float on over for a drink at the swim-up bar, located poolside.

If you are looking for activities, Getaway Cancun has them. Two pools provide plenty of area to play and swim in, and if you would like to sooth your troubles away, then jump into one of the four available jacuzzis. Fun not only can be found in everything that surrounds you, but can also be found on the tennis court. Bicycling, exercise room, dancing, outdoor theater, and shuttle buses into Cancun are all options available to keep boredom away.

Blue Bay Resorts

CONTACT:

WEBSITE:
www.bluebayresorts.com

EMAIL:
hotetur@hotetur.com

PHONE:
01-998-848-7900
or 800-215-1000 (US)

FAX:
01-998-848-794

All Blue Bay Resorts offer special honeymoon packages. Imagine your honeymoon surrounded by beautiful tropical gardens, sun, sand and everything in one place! Sounds like heaven, doesn't it?

SERVICES: Services vary at each of the Blue Bay Resorts. However, all offer pools, water-sports, tennis courts, exercise rooms or gyms, and multiple bars.

DINING: All meals are included and are served in a number of restaurants within the resorts. Typically, there are three or four restaurants per resort location. Getaway Cancun offers four. Snacks are also available.

RATES: Rates vary depending on destination. Call or email for details.

Resorts

Palm Island

St. Vincent and the Grenadines, West Indies

Crystal clear waters, towering palms, warm ocean breezes, and bright sunshine awaits guests of Palm Island. With the magnificent background of the West Indies as its setting, there will be no disappointments here.

Guests are lavished with everything they need to enjoy this all-inclusive island retreat. Rooms offer a variety of décor, however all rooms include an in-room safe, refrigerator, air conditioning, bathrobes, and room service for breakfast and high tea.

How would you like to spend your vacation alongside a pool with a free flowing waterfall? You can here and more! Bicycling, hiking, table tennis, horseshoes, and tennis are available activities. Day sailing trips provide for sightseeing on the islands of Tobago Cays, Union Island, Petit St. Vincent, and Mayreau. For an additional fee, guests may book scuba diving adventures, charter a boat, or experience the thrill that only deep-sea fishing can provide.

An intimate dinner for two can be enjoyed in any one of three separate locations. Evening dining consists of fresh fruits, vegetables and other ingredients found locally and prepared with an international flare. If a more casual style meal is desired the Palm Island Beach Club offers their beachside restaurant and bar. Evening brings entertainment such as beach barbecues and punch parties. If you prefer, how about a moonlit stroll along the white sand beaches. Romance is in the air everywhere at Palm Island.

SERVICES: Swimming can be enjoyed in the freshwater pool. Bicycling, hiking, walking trails, horseshoes, table tennis, tennis, boat trips, game room, and beach walking are activities included in your stay. Boat charters, snorkeling, scuba diving and deep-sea fishing are available nearby at an additional cost. A special wedding package is available or free with a 13-night stay and their Platinum Plan.

DINING: All meals and drinks are included and offer fresh fruits and vegetables prepared along with other local favorites in an international style. Three restaurants provide private, intimate atmospheres. Two bars serve an array of beverages.

RATES: 40 rooms are available with seasonal rates ranging from $680.00 to $870.00. A minimum stay is required and based on season. Children under the age of 16 years are permitted certain times of the year.

Secrets Excellence Resort

Punta Cana, Dominican Republic

This all-inclusive resort extends over an isolated stretch of beach on the Bavaro coastal region of the Caribbean. The resort has 446 suites spread through 13 buildings and offer four levels of suites. Each suite provide guests a jacuzzi, stocked mini-bar, satellite television, canopy beds, air-conditioning, safety

deposit boxes and a balcony just to mention a few of the amenities. Each suite offers a spectacular view of the ocean and beach, the mountains or plush gardens.

During the day many relax at poolside to work on their tan or take a cool dip and enjoy a refreshing beverage at one of the swim-up pool bars. The resort offers live entertainment and a casino. For those that are looking for something a little more romantic maybe you'll enjoy watching the sun set into the ocean horizon while you enjoy a seaside candle light romantic dinner. End the night by taking a moonlit horseback ride up and down the beach while you listen to the soothing sound of waves breaking on the cool wet sand just below.

SERVICES: Secrets Excellence Beach & Spa Resort is all-inclusive and goes all out. Your rates include a full service spa that offers steam baths, both a warm and cold whirlpool, use of fitness center, deep cleansing treatment, body mud treatment, waxing, beauty salon, exfoliation, manicures and pedicures and Swedish massage just to name a few of the services. There are also a wide variety of non-motorized water sports like windsurfing, sailing, snorkeling, catamarans, boogie boards, scuba diving, water polo and paddleboats. Some of the daytime land activities include tennis, archery, various tours, billiards, basketball, beach football, yoga, darts and horseback riding. These just give an idea of a long list of activities to keep you enthused. The resort also has nightly entertainment and shows, a disco and an onsite casino for those that like to gamble.

DINING: If you like food, this is the place for you. From Asian to Italian to a Texas-style steakhouse, you'll be sure to find something that pleases your palate. The resort host seven restaurants, nine bars and two lounges. They also offer 24-hour room service if you're in the mood for a late night snack.

RATES: Room rates per person per night range from $150.00 to $400.00 and varies seasonally.

Secrets Excellence Resort

CONTACT:

WEBSITE:
www.secretsresorts.com

EMAIL:
secretsresorts@secretsresorts.com

PHONE:
866-GO-SECRETS or 809-685-9880

FAX:
809-685-9990

ADDRESS:
Secrets Excellence Resort
Uvero Alto, Punt Cana
Provincia L Altagracia
Republica Dominicana

Grand Lido Braco

Jamaica

This resort is one in a chain of three all-inclusive resorts. It is, however the only one that offers a completely separate area and accommodations for those who desire a clothes free vacation.

Offering a 52 room separate unit that allows guests to go without tethers, Grand Lido Braco has a completely private nude beach facility that includes the Neptune Bar. The resort also offers the best of the best in amenities, all of which are included in the stay. Other rooms are also available to those who are not so adventurous. All rooms include air conditioning, coffeemaker, CD player, hair dryer, safe, iron and ironing board, and satellite television.

Activities and facilities include a spa that offers relaxing massages, facials, wraps, waxes, and other services. The fitness center allows guests to enjoy a vigorous workout. An on-premises beauty salon is always waiting to serve guests' needs. For those who wish a physical vacation, activities include hiking, bicycling, volleyball, a nine hole golf course on the grounds with an 18-hole course located nearby with all green fees included, three tennis courts, and four jacuzzis may also be enjoyed.

Meals and everything one can drink are included. The five dining facilities allow guests to dine as formal or casual as they desire. Offering a wide variety of foods, from Jamaican to Japanese, the restaurants are sure to provide a meal to satisfy. After dinner, the nightlife begins. A piano bar and disco offers two different styles of fun. Nightly theme parties are also provided. Late night snacks are available outside the disco and the Neptune Bar is ready to serve those who would like to enjoy the evening, au naturel.

Grand Lido Braco's sister resorts are also adult only facilities and offer clothing optional beaches. They are Grand Lido Negril and Grand Lido San Souci. Each is as magnificent as the Grand Lido Braco.

If you are looking for a vacation that will allow you to stay in an accommodating facility, then book your next trip and stay at Grand Lido Braco.

Grand Lido Braco

CONTACT:

WEBSITE:
www.superclubs.com

EMAIL:
info@superclubs.com

PHONE:
877-GO SUPER (467-8737)

FAX:
954-925-0334

SERVICES: 24-hour room service is available to guests as are three tennis courts, four jacuzzis, beach services, hiking, spa, bicycling, beauty salon, fitness center, nine hole onsite golf course, local 18-hole golf course with all green fees included, sauna, volleyball, and soccer field.

DINING: Five dining facilities serve meals with flavors from Jamaican to Japanese, and allow guests to enjoy formal to casual dining experiences. Several bars provide drinks and entertainment. One bar allows guests to socialize au naturel.

RATES: Call, visit their website, or email for details and current rates.

Patos Planet

Nicoya Peninsula, Costa Rica

Nestled on a hillside with the sound of waves crashing the shoreline lies one of the loveliest spots any adult could ask for in a vacation retreat. And being an adult only, clothing optional facility (membership required for duration of stay), guests can fulfill their deepest vacation fantasies.

This truly exotic location allows for some very erotic and intimate moments to be shared, either as a couple or with others desiring the same experiences. Activities include horseback riding, snorkeling, tennis, nature hiking, fishing, and canoeing. There are also special events that may be planned according to guests' taste. Dining enjoyments can be found at the restaurant located at Patos Planet or other options are available locally in the nearby village. All memberships include accommodations, meals, non-alcoholic drinks, and airport transportation.

Because of the relaxed nature of this facility, guests should all go with an open mind and an understanding of the nature of those that visit here. Only adults 18 years of age or older will be accommodated. Activities may or may not include multiple couples, however it is not out of the question at Patos Planet. As long as all parties are agreeable to situations, it is up to guests as to what desires may be fulfilled. This just might be the vacation of your dreams.

Resorts

CONTACT:

WEBSITE:
www.patos.com

EMAIL:
PlanetPatoCR@aol.com
(English & Spanish)
Planet@patos.com
(Italian, German & French)

SERVICES: Guests may enjoy horseback riding, fishing, canoeing, snorkeling, tennis, and beach golf all in a natural atmosphere.

DINING: Meals are provided at the retreat with other meal options available locally in the nearby village.

RATES: $195.00 a day per couple to $1250.00 a week per couple and $145.00 a day single to $900.00 a week per single. Email or visit their website for more details.

Resorts

Atlantic Shores Resort

Key West, Florida

Key West is known as one of the party capitals of the world, and for good reason. They have great weather, friendly people, and some very exciting party spots for adults. Atlantic Shores Resort is just such a place.

The resort is world renown for their clothing optional pool and deck area. Even though it is clothing optional, most people opt not to let their clothes get in the way of a good time. Locals as well as tourists bare it all around the oceanfront pool area enjoying the warm Florida sunshine and a few cocktails while making new friends or partying with old ones.

Atlantic Shores Resort is located in the heart of Old Town on South Street right between Duval and Simonton. Duval Street is the main drag where you will find most of the party spots. Duval Street is also known as the longest street in the world because it connects the Gulf of Mexico and the Atlantic Ocean.

This is an oceanfront resort that sports a tropical art deco look. All of its 72 rooms feature custom-made art deco furnishings. Most likely though, you won't be spending much time indoors. Every Sunday night the resort presents it's now famous Tea by the Sea party. This is a party that welcomes all lifestyles and recently celebrated its 15th anniversary. There is also the popular Cinema Shores on Thursday evenings where you can watch a movie outdoors on the big movie screen, while laying back in your lounge chair, sipping drinks, and munching on the free popcorn. There are many choices for nearby dining, but the resort also offers some tasty treats at their Diner Shores Restaurant.

The resort host 72 rooms. Each room has air-conditioning, a coffee maker, ceiling fans, telephone, safety deposit box, private bathroom, a clock radio and cable television. The suites also come equipped with a microwave, refrigerator, VCR and most have a private balcony.

Key West has many great things to see and do. If you would like to learn more about Key West and some of the area attractions, they have many good resources at www.keywest.com. Key West is also the home of the famous and usually revealing Fantasy Fest in October.

If you check out their website, they have a virtual tour that you can take of the pool and deck area. While it is a neat feature, nothing compares to being there. If you enjoy partying in a casual environment with a lot of naked women and men, you'll want to plan your visit soon.

Atlantic Shores Resort

CONTACT:

WEBSITE:
www.atlanticshoresresort.com

EMAIL:
info@atlanticshoresresort.com

PHONE:
800-598-6988 or 305-296-2491

ADDRESS:
Atlantic Shores Resort
510 South Street
Key West, Florida 33040

SERVICES: Clothing-optional sunning deck, pier and pool. The famous Tea by the Sea party and Cinema Shores events are on Thursday evenings. A wide variety of water activities are available. There are wave runners, para-sail rides, sailboats, snorkel, dive trips, fishing trips, sunset sails. Gambling trips, historic tours by Old Town Trolley Tours and much more can also be arranged for your pleasure.

DINING: The Diner Shores Restaurant has a wide variety of dishes. They serve breakfast, lunch and dinner. They are open from 7:30am to 4:00am. The pool bar and grill serves food from 11:00am to 5:00pm. There is also a full service bar located on-site. A party store is just across the street and there are a variety of restaurants within walking distance of the resort.

RATES: 72 rooms. Prices range from $99.00 for an efficiency to $250.00 for a queen. Price varies depending on time of year.

Resorts

Rio Caliente

Primevera, Mexico

Does the stress in life have you down? Has it tugged and pulled at your relationship, health, and mind? Then try a vacation that is truly different. Take a trip on the healthy side at Rio Caliente for a healthy, hot springs, and spa vacation that will renew your body, mind, soul, and relationship.

Sitting on an extinct volcanic area of Mexico, Rio Caliente is a treat guests will never forget. Accommodations are quaint cottages, decorated with a Mexican flare, and have cozy fireplaces that add rich warmth to the room. Guests are provided private baths, with either a shower or a tub and decorated nicely in beautiful tile. Sundecks for each cottage allow for a private and quiet sit in the Mexican sunlight. Public telephone, fax services, public access email, VCR, and satellite television are available within the vacation facility, but are not offered in the cottages.

An extensive list of special treatments is provided at an additional, affordable cost. Mud wraps, foot reflexology, manicures, pedicures, facials, scalp treatments, anti-aging therapy, anti-stress therapy, and numerous types of massages are at the beck and call of the guests of Rio Caliente.

Activities are endless. Two heated lap pools, two private his and her plunge pools, and a steam room allow guests to refresh and sooth the stress from their lives. For those with a physical endurance, hiking, horseback riding, Yoga, and Tai Chi are offered. A shopping or sightseeing trip into one of Mexico's favorite areas can be a relaxing way to spend the day.

To replenish the fuels needed for all this fun, gourmet, fat free meals are served. Items such as fresh squeezed juices, homemade breads and granola, and eggs highlight breakfasts. Lunch brings a variety of salads, rice, breads, and fruits. Dinner meals are just as healthy as their predecessors offering soups, salads, tostados, tortillas, fresh fruits, and juices. Because of the emphasis on low fat foods, no meats are served at Rio Caliente.

A romantic, moonlit dip in the pool or a casual soak in the eight-person whirlpool or hot tub is just the ticket to end a rejuvenating day of relaxation and fun.

For anyone looking for a very different, yet completely relaxing and healthy, vacation getaway, and still be able to enjoy the flavor of a different land, Rio Caliente is the place to go. Runaway to Rio Caliente!

Rio Caliente

CONTACT:

WEBSITE:
www.riocaliente.com

EMAIL:
riocal@aol.com

PHONE:
650-615-9543 or 800-200-2927
(Reservations only)

FAX:
650-615-0601

ADDRESS:
U.S. Office
Rio Caliente
P.O. Box 897
Millbrae, California 94030

SERVICES: Lap pools, plunge pools, eight-person whirlpool, hot tub, hiking, Yoga, Tai Chi, steam room, television, fax, phone, and public email access are some of the services offered to guests. Other services offered at an affordable additional expense are numerous forms of massage, facials, manicures, pedicures, therapies, scalp treatments, shopping trips, sightseeing trips, and horseback riding.

DINING: Meals provided are fat free and offer many home-made items including breads and fresh squeezed juices. Breakfast, lunch, and dinner are served, however, due to the emphasis on fat free, no meats are offered.

RATES: Special packages are offered and rates vary. Call or email for details.

Resorts

Exotic Caye Beach Resort

Ambergris Caye, Belize

Resting alongside crystal clear waters and among towering palms lays the Exotic Caye Beach Resort in Belize. Refreshing tropical breezes blow and bright sunshine reflects enticingly off the pristine white beaches.

Exotic Caye Beach Resort offers only the best! Their suites are private and located oceanfront with an outstanding view. The luxurious suites are really a home away from home during your stay. You can even create a sumptuous meal for that special person in your life in the privacy of your own suite, as each is fully equipped with a kitchen. Groceries may be found at one of the local markets just walking distance from the resort.

Experience the adventure of the seas, diving or snorkeling off the coast of Ambergris Caye. Quench the archeologist in you by touring the Mayan ruins. Hitting a hole-in-one may not be out of the question at the private golf course. Manatees reside locally and watching them is an avid activity that will peak your interests in the strange and exotic creatures. Other activities include river trips, sunset cruises, kayaking, windsurfing, museum tours, horseback riding, and canoe trips.

Does your mind say, "Gone fishing"? It can and will at Exotic Caye Beach Resort. Deep-sea fishing excursions are available year round. Imagine landing that big sailfish or king mackerel. Marlin abounds all year long. Other fishing can be found from the shores of the island. Grouper, snapper, and barracuda are all possible catches right from the shoreline. For those that prefer fly-fishing, there are options available to you as well.

If you are looking for relaxation, try a Swedish massage, aromatherapy, herbal body treatment, body wrap, or facial massage. All of these services are offered at Exotic Caye Beach Resort for an additional cost. Soak up some rays poolside or help yourself to a refreshing dip.

Dining enjoyments abound. If you do not wish to cook your own meals, then try one of the many local restaurants. Dining options include fresh seafood, Italian fare, Chinese selections, and of course Belize favorites. Your taste buds will enjoy the vacation too!

Nightlife also abounds on Ambergris Caye. Visit the Pier Lounge, Big Daddy's, or Tarzan's for live entertainment and dancing. If its music you like, you are sure to find the type that suits your taste. Mexican, rock, and reggae are just a few of the musical styles that can be heard.

Take an adventurous, but relaxing trip to Ambergris Caye, Belize and stay at the Exotic Caye Beach Resort. It is a dream vacation come true!

Exotic Caye Beach Resort

CONTACT:

WEBSITE:
www.belizeisfun.com

EMAIL:
playador@btl.net

PHONE:
800-201-9389 (US only)

FAX:
770-974-6414

ADDRESS:
Ambergris Caye
Belize, Central America

SERVICES: Maid and laundry services are provided at the resort. Suites are completely equipped. Adventures in fishing, water sports, touring, boating, and sightseeing can be found either at the resort or locally. A swimming pool, private golf course, and dive shop is also available at the resort.

DINING: Breakfast, lunch, and dinner can be prepared in the fully equipped in-suite kitchens, or a wide variety of restaurants are available for your dining pleasures.

RATES: Complete, fully equipped suites are offered at seasonal rates. Specially priced packages are also offered. Call for more details.

Resorts

Vatulele Island Resort

Vatulele, Fiji

Winner of the 2000 Small Luxury Hotel of the Year Award, Vatulele is an intimate and luxurious vacation experience that is also warm and friendly. Vatulele is one of the small islands in Fiji and, as such, is a quiet location with tall palms and sandy beaches, surrounded by stunningly beautiful azure waters.

While at the resort, you'll stay in one of only 15 thatched roof villas on the island spaced about 150 feet apart to provide privacy amid a thriving natural jungle setting. While it's an exciting experience for the adventurer, it may not be for those desiring a high-rise hotel experience. Each villa has a private dressing area and comfortable sleeping quarters featuring a king size bed, as well as a roomy living area and private bath with shower. All meals are included in your stay and most are served outdoors to take advantage of the nearly perfect weather. In the cooler months of June, July, and August, you may want a sweater to wear as you dine under the stars. All food is carefully prepared with gourmet details and a focus on fresh seafood. To ensure quality, ingredients are flown in daily from Australia and New Zealand. Vatulele is also proud of their impressive wine cellar featuring limitless French champagne to indulge its guests. Wine lovers rejoice!

Daily activities at Vatulele Island Resort reflect both the relaxed pace of the Fiji islands and the commitment of the owners to making sure its guests are comfortable and entertained. The beaches lend themselves to swimming, sunning, snorkeling and exploring for hours on end, and for experienced divers, there are also a number of diving excursions available for a fee.

If you're thinking about getting married, the resort provides complete wedding services. This unique wedding is usually held at sunset in a tropical church. In their native dress, Fijian warriors bring the bride to the church in a flower-decorated boat. Flower petals line the beach as she is carried ashore to take her vows. The package includes a 20-plus person Fijian choir, with singers and dancers, champagne, an informal wedding cake, the floral decorations and the minister.

The Point is the resort's exclusive suite that was open in June of 2002. This two- story private villa has its own private pool, wine cellar, sun deck, view of the beach and ocean and a staff of professionals to wait on your every need and desire.

Vatulele Island Resort

CONTACT:

WEBSITE:
www.vatulele.com

EMAIL:
vatulele@is.com.fj

PHONE:
800-828-9146 (North America) or 679-550-300

FAX:
679-550-262

ADDRESS:
Vatulele Island Resort
Vatulele, Fiji

SERVICES: All water sports except scuba are included in the cost of your room. A variety of scuba excursions are available for a fee.

DINING: All meals and beverages including alcoholic beverages are included in your room price.

RATES: The per night rate for a couple is $1125.00. A four-night minimum stay is required. Double occupancy is standard, but singles are allowed by application for $675.00 per night and an extra person may be allowed in the room by application for an additional $330.00 per night. Children under 12 are not permitted except for two weeks out of the year.

Resorts

Galley Bay

Antigua, West Indies

Surrounded by the turquoise waters of the Caribbean Sea, the island of Antigua is home to Galley Bay. This all-inclusive luxury resort is designed to make your stay on the island unforgettable. Each of the resort's 70 guest rooms offer air conditioning, ceiling fans, tiled floors, bathrobes, coffee machines, an in-room safe, king size beds, private baths, and a balcony or patio. Choose from one of several accommodation styles.

The romantic Gauguin cottages are on the edge of a bird sanctuary lagoon just a few yards away from the beach. These cottages consist of two thatched-roof huts connected by a breezeway, one serving as a bedroom and the other as a dressing room. Rooms are located directly on the beach and offer seaside patios. Available two-story rooms are more spacious than the standard beach front rooms and offer walk-in closets and private balconies. For the ultimate in beach side luxury, stay in a premium beachfront suite. These deluxe accommodations offer over 700 square feet of space with patios, balconies, and fabulous ocean views.

All meals are included in your stay, so start your day at the Sea Grape Restaurant for a sumptuous breakfast. This beach side restaurant serves award-winning meals a la carte for breakfast, lunch, and dinner. After breakfast, head to the beach for windsurfing, sailing, snorkeling, and kayaking. All equipment and instruction for these activities is complimentary. When you've had enough of the saltwater, take a dip in the resort's huge freeform freshwater swimming pool. This cool and refreshing structure has the look and feel of a real lagoon and includes a spectacular waterfall.

For lunch and dinner, you'll have to decide whether to go back to the Sea Grape, or try Gauguin Restaurant for a more casual meal. Early evening is a good time to stop by the Teepee Bar to enjoy hors d'oeuvres and your favorite beverage. After dinner, try the lounge bar for that perfect drink to finish off your perfect day.

If you're only staying a few days, you'll probably stay very busy just trying to do everything available at the resort, but for a longer stay you may want to consider arranging an outing. The resort staff can help you pick from several day tours around beautiful Antigua including shopping, golf, historical island tours and more. If you'd like to go exploring on your own, arrangements can be made for a rental car as well.

Galley Bay

CONTACT:

WEBSITE:
www.classicislandresorts.com

EMAIL:
bayres@antigua-resorts.com

PHONE:
954-481-8787 or
800-345-0356(Reservations)

FAX:
954-481-1661

ADDRESS:
Galley Bay
P.O. Box 305, St. John's
Antigua, West Indies

SERVICES: Snorkeling, windsurfing, kayaking, tennis, and croquet are all available onsite. For an additional charge, guests can arrange island tours shopping excursions, golf, rental cars, massage, and a variety of other services on the island.

DINING: Galley Bay is all-inclusive, so all meals and beverages, including alcoholic beverages, are included. The resort offers two restaurants, a lounge bar and a beachside bar.

RATES: Per night room rates are from $550.00 to $730.00 in summer, $670.00 to $850.00 in winter and from $770.00 to $1000.00 during the holidays.

Resorts

Beaches Resorts

Caribbean

From the creators of the world famous Sandals Resorts, comes Beaches Resorts. With two, adult only 16 years of age or older, all-inclusive locations, Beaches Resorts can have you basking in luxury and sunshine in no time. Beaches Royal Plantation is an architectural delight. Taking you back to pre-civil war times with its southern plantation design. But this resort is by no means old.

Royal Plantation offers 80 lavishly decorated suites fit for "The Donald" himself. Executive luxuries you would never expect, these suites are equipped with Internet service, fax and phones located in the living room, bedroom, and bath. They also contain a high quality bar, guest robes, cable television, VCR, CD player, and in-room safe.

Guests may enjoy all the activities associated with a beach resort such as golf, volleyball, scuba diving, snorkeling, sun bathing, swimming pool or beach swimming, steam bath, jacuzzis, European style spa, and local tours.

Gourmet meals wait to delight you at any one of the three Royal Plantation gourmet restaurants. Serving only the finest foods, guests are sure to enjoy a meal fit for a king! Drinks run endlessly at Royal Plantation and are included in your stay. If privacy is the mood, then guests may order from the 24-hour room service that is available and also included.

Royal Plantation is host to five pools with in-pool swim up lounges, twelve miles of bleached sandy beach and nine restaurants. Complete unlimited use of the golf facilities at the nearby Sandals Golf & Country Club is also included.

If there is not enough at the resort to keep you occupied,

scuba diving with professional lead instruction is included in your stay at all of the Beaches Resorts. Full on-site spa services are offered. For something really different, take a trip on the glass bottom boat and see what is really under the sea without having to dive.

Beaches Resorts

CONTACT:

WEBSITE:
www.beaches.com

EMAIL:
info@beaches.com

PHONE:
888-BEACHES (232-2437)

Beaches also offers their Grande Sport Resort at Ciboney. This resort is equally as impressive and only accommodates adults 16 years of age or older, both couples and singles. Grande Sport sits on 50 acres and has 90 fresh water pools...yes 90! There is also a rock climbing wall, a belted trampoline, full sports facilities, complete spa services and has its own 18 hole, par 72 championship golf course. Live entertainment is provided nightly at one of the five-onsite bars.

All Beaches Resorts offer their Blue Chip Hurricane Guarantee, ensuring quality and service should Mother Nature interrupt your trip. Don't take a chance, step into the VIP treatment at Beaches Resorts and rest assured, your trip is guaranteed!

SERVICES: Pools, lavish white beaches, in-room jacuzzi, swimming, waterskiing, tours, tennis, shopping, fitness center, glass bottom boat tours, and much more are provided by Beaches Resorts.

DINING: Gourmet dining at its best at any of the three in-house gourmet restaurants. Drinks are included and can be served either poolside, beachside, or in the bar. You set the limits on drinks!

RATES: Rates are seasonal but range from $310.00 to $1150.00 per night per person. Call or email for details.

Resorts

Bear Trail Couples Resort

Whitney, Ontario, Canada

From cozy log cottages just for two, to luxurious honeymoon suites with over 1,000 square feet of space, to a set of suites which can be combined into 2,800 square feet of vacation enjoyment, Bear Trail Resort is sure to have accommodations right for you. All are thoughtfully decorated and have varying amenities such as fireplaces, hot tubs, and porches. Each room comes with a TV, VCR, coffee maker, refrigerator, clock radio, iron, hairdryer, and snuggly robes. Breakfast and dinner are included in your stay and are served in their elegantly appointed dining room. Cuisine is focused on non-gourmet, country-style cooking. Lunch is also available for an additional charge and, in the warm summer months, is available on the outside patio.

The property is adjacent to both Algonquin Park and Galeairy Lake making it a nature lover's paradise. Both of these natural wonders provide plenty to see and explore during your stay. Use the inn's complimentary mountain bikes to explore one of the many trails in the park or take a slower pace on foot. In winter, breathe the crisp air as you ski through the park. At Bear Trail Couples Resort, skis, skates, and snowshoes are provided to guests. For summer fun on the lake, take advantage of free water-skiing, tubing, sailing, and wind surfing. If you just want to lounge in the out of doors, the property offers you a 5,000 square foot, multi level patio with large hot tub, heated saltwater pool, and a diving deck extending out into the lake.

SERVICES: A variety of sporting equipment for all seasons is included in the price of your room. During the months without snow, room service is complimentary. Spa treatments are available for a fee. The resort also has a large recreation room with billiard tables, ping-pong, shuffleboard, darts, and foosball. Drinks can be ordered to the recreation room. An intimate resort accommodating up to 48 couples.

DINING: A large breakfast is served each day until 10:30am. Dinner service is featured in an elegant dining room. There are many main course choices per night each served with homemade soup, salad and desserts. Dinner also features a wide variety of vintage wines from around the world. There is an on-site bar that is open until 10:00pm nightly.

RATES: Rates range from $70.00 to $259.00 per person, per night depending on the type of room and time of year you travel.

Bear Trail Couples Resort

CONTACT:

WEBSITE:
www.beartrailresort.com

EMAIL:
info@beartrailresort.com

PHONE:
(001) 613-637-2662

FAX:
(001) 613-637-2615

ADDRESS:
Bear Trail Couples Resort
P.O. Box 310, Galeairy Lake Road
Whitney (Algonquin Park), Ontario
Canada K0J 2M0

Lifestyles Resort & Spa

Manzanillo, Mexico

ifestyles Resort & Spa is perched on a cliff overlooking the Pacific Ocean on Tenacatita Bay. The grounds are covered in beautiful gardens surrounded by lush vegetation and magnificent floras will take your breath away. It is not uncommon to see dolphins jumping on the horizon right from your room.

Open-minded guests will find an endless list of things to do here. Sun worshipping on the clothing optional secluded beach, taking a dip in the topless swimming pool or maybe relaxing in one of the two hot tubs that are hanging over the bay are among some of the favorite things you'll enjoy. The 24 villa style rooms offer comfortable accommodations for members of any lifestyle. The atmosphere allows guests the freedom to be themselves without all the trappings of outside life. Numerous local shops wait to be browsed by visitors. Dining facilities, beach combing, fishing and local events will entertain those that wish to venture outside the private grounds.

Put your bags together, but pack light for this adult only destination. It's the ultimate in relaxation and you won't be in need of too many things here! It is a paradise resort every naturalist has been looking for. If you are a nudist at heart, give Lifestyles Resort & Spa and their clothing optional lifestyle a try.

If you're looking for something a little larger but just as adventurous, check out Lifestyles Resort & Spas larger sister resort Desire Resort & Spa. Desire Resort & Spa offer couples an opportunity to fulfill their romantic as well as their erotic fantasies.

SERVICES: A wide array of activities are available including tennis, horseback riding and yoga lessons. There is also a fully equipped fitness center, beauty salon, boutique and nightclub to keep you occupied. The resort has a full service spa with sauna, steam room and indoor jacuzzi.

DINING: Breakfast, lunch and gourmet dinner is served outside on a covered deck overlooking the ocean. The onsite bar creates the perfect romantic setting to relax or enjoy your favorite drink.

RATES: 24 rooms allow for a smaller guest list ensuring private fun and enjoyment. Rates are all-inclusive and start at $150.00 per person, per night.

Lifestyles Resort & Spa

CONTACT:

WEBSITE:
www.lifestyles-resorts.com

EMAIL:
manzanillo@lifestyles-resorts.com

PHONE:
866-807-5205 (US) or 714-503-6138

FAX:
714-821-9919

ADDRESS:
Lifestyles Resort & Spa
Km. 20 Carretera Federal 200
Tenacatita, Jalisco, México
C. P. 48989

Club Ambiance

St. Ann, Jamaica

Kick back in a relaxing and easy-going atmosphere that is tropically ideal, Club Ambiance, Jamaica. This adult retreat

pampers you in style, while allowing you to completely feel at home. Rooms are light and breezy and provide a king size or two double beds, in-room safe, telephone, hairdryer, satellite television, full private bath, iron, ironing board, air conditioning, and a view to die for!

The indoor and outdoor restaurants both serve delicious meals with either Caribbean or international flavor. A dining terrace allows for meals to be enjoyed outdoors under a big, beautiful sky. Five bars provide all the drinks you could ever want.

Pass the days away on a bicycle tour, playing shuffleboard, snorkeling or pedal boating. Maybe you would prefer to take

diving lessons at the five star diving school. The Ocean Club has activities for those who prefer to remain indoors. Enjoy pool, darts, indoor games or the big screen TV.

A shopping excursion can be the time of your life in nearby Ocho Rios, or you can tee off at the local golf course. Rafting, museums, and horseback riding are also located nearby.

Nightlife includes theme nights, disco and dancing to the music provided by the resident band at Club Ambiance.

A wedding chapel located on the premises provides a quaint and cozy place to tie the knot. Club Ambiance can help with all the arrangements to satisfy the legal requirements and your

dreams! Plus, they offer wedding and honeymoon pack-ages that will make your wedding trip the best time of your life! Club Ambiance, Jamaica is an ocean-side dream vacation destination!

SERVICES: Guests can enjoy snorkeling, swimming, boating, massages, manicures, pedicures, exercise room, bicy-cling tours, shopping excursions, local museums, local golf facilities, horseback riding at nearby facility, car rental, diving school, dancing, and many other local options available.

Club Ambiance

CONTACT:

WEBSITE:
www.clubambiance.com

EMAIL:
info@clubambiance.com

PHONE:
800-822-3274 or 876-973-4705

FAX:
876-973-2067

ADDRESS:
Club Ambiance
P.O. Box 20
Runaway Bay, St. Ann, Jamaica,
West Indies

DINING: Breakfast and lunch buffets are served at Café Calypso and evening meals may be enjoyed at the Seaside Terrace. All meals and beverages are included with your room rate.

RATES: 100 rooms are available with seasonal rates, starting at $95.00 to $160.00 per night. Honeymoon packages range from $790.00 to $1700.00. Wedding packages are also available. Call or email for details.

Turtle Island

Turtle Island, Fiji

At Turtle Island in Fiji, you'll quickly realize that this resort is designed to be the ultimate romantic island retreat for lovers. You'll arrive at Turtle Island by seaplane to discover a land free from hustle and bustle—there aren't even any TVs here. What you will find are tall palm trees, pristine beaches, skies that stretch forever, and water beyond description. Here you are free to focus solely on your companion and your own relaxation. You'll stay in one of a mere 14 bures, or cottages, built by Fijian craftsman of native woods. These accommodations are primitive enough to blend seamlessly into their surroundings, but offer total comfort to guests. Each one has a welcoming four-poster bed, ceiling fans,

a terrace, a separate living area, a personal safe, a stocked wet bar area, and a private bath with spa tub. Each outdoor terrace has a shower for washing off sand and seawater to ensure your comfort once you've stepped inside your cozy retreat.

The most natural activity on Turtle Island is anything centered on the 14 beaches. Swim, snorkel, scuba, lounge . . . simply take in the incredible

Resorts

beauty. Divers will be enchanted with the vibrant reefs around the island and snorkelers will marvel at the many species of marine life swimming just a few feet from the beach. For more private endeavors, you'll be pleased to find that many of the island's beaches are private and secluded. You can arrange a private picnic on one of these beaches and enjoy your after picnic privacy with a skinny dip in the crystal clear waters. You can also arrange for a picnic on the beach outside your bure if you like.

Meals at Turtle Island are as pleasing to the palate as the scenery is to the eyes. Each meal is large and sumptuous. Breakfasts are largely traditional, although a few exotic choices are available. Lunch and dinner feature a kaleidoscope of fresh seafood options, as well as decadent desserts such as Chocolate Trio and Toasted Brioche, and wine lovers will find themselves quite pleased with the resort's extensive wine list.

CONTACT:

WEBSITE:
www.turtlefiji.com

EMAIL:
usa@turtlefiji.com

PHONE:
877-2-TURTLE or 360-256-4347

FAX:
360-253-3934

ADDRESS:
Turtle Island
10906 NE 39th St.
Quad 205 Suite A-I
Vancouver, Washington 98682-6789

SERVICES: Your hosts can arrange a variety of land and sea activities including horse back riding, sunset cruises, a champagne picnic lunch and others.

DINING: The restaurant at Turtle Island features a top notch menu that's available for viewing on their website. There's something for everyone at every meal, but  there is an emphasis on fresh seafood and local produce for obvious reasons. The wine list is extensive.

RATES: Rates for All-Inclusive Deluxe Bure Packages start at $1090.00 per couple per day.

Resorts

Harmony Club Resort

Paget Parish, Bermuda

Harmony Club Resort is the only all-inclusive resort available on the island of Bermuda. An upscale and elegant

resort, Harmony Club offers 68 guest rooms in five charming buildings, each built in the traditional English style that typifies the island. The romantic grounds provide an inspiring setting for couples, young and old. Paget Manor, the resort's

original structure, offers several rooms with hard wood floors over looking your choice of the freshwater pool or tennis courts.

The Bougainvillea, Suet, and Wild Poppy buildings are a good choice for golfers because of their close proximately to the put-

ting greens. These buildings have tiled floors and balconies on the second floor. The Sunrise building is on the east side of the property. All rooms have private bath and shower, heat and air conditioners, safes, satellite TV, coffee and tea makers, bathrobes, alarm clocks, direct dial telephones, and an assortment of toiletries.

The elegant buildings and lushly landscaped gardens of the Harmony Club Resort sit just a seven-minute walk from lovely Stonington Beach. If you don't feel like walking, hop on board a motor scooter provided by the resort and reach the beach in about a minute. The front desk

will supply you with passes that provide you with complimentary extras at Stonington Beach including towels, chairs, umbrellas, and changing rooms.

Start your day with a hearty breakfast buffet at Casuarina Restaurant served 7:00am to 10:00am daily. The chef will cook your eggs to order upon your arrival. A light lunch is served in the Bay Grape Lounge from 12:00pm to 3:00pm and dinner is back at the Casuarina Restaurant to sample the chef's specialties along with a glass of house white or red wine. Dress in the dining facilities is generally casual, but on Sundays gentlemen are asked to wear a jacket. End your days with dancing to live music

Harmony Club Resort

CONTACT:

WEBSITE:
www.harmonyclub.com

EMAIL:
reservations@harmonyclub.com or
email@harmonyclub.com

PHONE:
888-427-6664 or 800-869-5824

FAX:
441-236-2624

ADDRESS:
Harmony Club
South Shore Road
Paget Parish 03, Bermuda

provided at the Bay Grape Lounge.

If you choose to explore Bermuda during your stay at the Harmony Club Resort, your hosts can arrange for a variety of tours including shopping, horseback riding, and historical tours of the centuries-old forts and churches on the island. Golf packages are also available.

SERVICES: Nightly entertainment is provided. A golf package including daily green fees is available for $70.00 per person per day. Other tours and activities can be arranged by the staff for an additional charge.

DINING: All meals and drinks are included in the package price. There is both a restaurant and lounge featuring a wide variety of foods. Themed buffets are served at various times throughout the week. A traditional English tea is served each afternoon consisting of teas, cakes, finger sandwiches, and cookies.

RATES: Rates are $635.00 per person for three nights, $841.00 per person for four nights, $1047.00 per person for five nights, $1253.00 per person for six nights, and $1459.00 per person for seven nights. Additional days are $206.00. All rates are based on double occupancy and adults only.

Viking's Exotic Resort

Dominican Republic, Caribbean

Imagine a beautiful exotic island paradise with an elegant villa full of stunningly beautiful women who are waiting to fulfill your fantasies in style. Single men and adventurous couples can enjoy this fantasy through a vacation experience from Viking's Exotic Resort.

Upon your arrival you'll enjoy a welcome cocktail party where you'll be introduced to Viking's lovely international models. You'll be able to meet with all the ladies and decide who you would like to have as your companion while staying at the resort.

The typical vacation experience from Viking is the four-day, three night package. Other popular options include the VIP Package as well as a Birthday Boy Package if you feel like indulging on your special day. What Viking offers is a luxury experience complete with gourmet meals, champagne, access to private beaches, horseback riding on the beach, and plenty of available water sports for added entertainment.

It's a true all-inclusive vacation package, but unlike other resorts, at Viking's you can also enjoy the companionship of beautiful models from such exotic places as Russia, Hungary, Venezuela and Brazil 24-hours a day. They are with you for your entire stay!

The cost for this level of luxury and companionship is $3900.00 for their standard package or up to $5900.00 for the VIP package. Viking's Exotic Resort also offers longer and

Resorts

shorter stays to fit with almost any desire and budget. Check out their website for more details.

SERVICES: Beautiful international models, companionship 24-hours a day, swimming, clothing optional areas, swimming pool and sun tanning. World-class golf, jet skis, ATV's, horseback riding, charter boats and excursions can also be enjoyed for an additional cost.

DINING: Gourmet food prepared daily by your personal chef. Enjoy island favorites as well as traditional meals. Special requests can be accommodated. All drinks including wine, premium liquors, beer and soft drinks are included.

RATES: Rates vary depending on selected package. Standard rates are $3900.00 for a four day, three-night all-inclusive package. Visit Viking's website for current rates and packages.

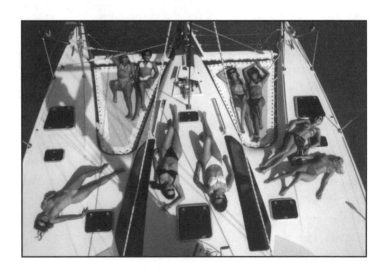

Strawberry Hill Resort

Irish Town, Jamaica

trawberry Hill is an exclusive mountain retreat just outside the coastal city of Kingston, Jamaica. This unique resort sits 3,000 feet above the city amid Jamaica's beautiful Blue Mountains. The property is lush and green and features several rooming options. You can opt to stay in a studio suite, a deluxe one bedroom, or even rent a whole house for you and your companion or a larger group. All are neatly decorated and feature stunning views of the landscape.

While enjoying the scenery, you'll have several options for both active and restful pursuits. Stay on the property and enjoy use of Strawberry Hill's pool, library, gym, and spa facilities. Take advantage of the elevation around the resort, which naturally lends itself to a variety of hiking and biking adventures from leisurely to challenging, venture out just a little further and take in the local beaches, or try your luck on one of the nearby golf courses.

Resorts

93

History buffs, culture lovers, and anyone staying more than a few days at Strawberry Hill should consider exploring Jamaica's capital city, Kingston. Tours of the city are available on which you can learn a great deal about the history, industry, and culture of the region. Don't forget to stop by nearby Port Royal—previously occupied by pirates when it was known as the most wicked port in the world. Of course, shoppers will also enjoy Kingston for the wide variety of goods to be found from all over the world at incredible prices.

The food at Strawberry Hill is recommended to all visitors of the area because of its reputation for high quality. Eat breakfast, lunch, and dinner onsite for a taste of new Jamaican cuisine, or venture out to the surrounding area to taste the wide variety of food available. If you love the nightlife, Kingston also has numerous bars and clubs to explore after dark.

SERVICES: Strawberry Hill offers spa facilities, a gift store, a gym, a library, limited conference facilities, and helicopter service to and from the airport. Your hosts can also direct you to a variety of available tours around the island.

DINING: Strawberry Hill has an onsite restaurant serving a continental breakfast, as well as lunch and dinner. The menu features new Jamaican cuisine.

RATES: Room rates per night are $325.00 to $775.00 and vary according to accommodations and time of year. All rates are based on single or double occupancy.

Kantenah Bay Riviera Maya, Mexico

El Dorado Resort & Spa is an all-inclusive exotic resort over-looking the beach of Mexico's Yucatan peninsula. The resort is spread across 40 acres covered in palm trees and lush tropical plants. With over one mile of warm white sand, the beach is covered with shaded lounge chairs where many guests find themselves relaxing if they are not in one of the two swimming pools.

All the rooms are located in separate two or three story buildings that face the ocean of the Mexican Caribbean. Each suite is equipped with air-conditioning, cable TV, radio, marble bathrooms, ceiling fans, a private terrace or patio with a hammock and some suites are available with a full size in-room jacuzzi. El Dorado Resort & Spa also offers a free wedding package. Call the resort for complete details.

SERVICES: A full service all-inclusive resort that offer guests plenty to keep you busy including tennis courts, use of snorkeling equipment, sauna and Turkish baths, steam room, fitness center, full service spa, outdoor jacuzzi, nightly entertainment, non-motorized water sports and a scuba clinic with certified diving instructors. The tour desk can make arrangements if you want to venture off-site. A daily shuttle runs into Playa del Carmen where you can take a guided tour of the Mayan ruins near the resort, visit the underground caves, go horseback riding, dive with the dolphins, go deep sea fishing, take in a round of golf or visit Xel-Ha's natural aquarium.

DINING: The resort houses three full service restaurants each with a different theme. Los Arrecifes features international cuisine and is open 24-hours. La Carreta offers

Resorts

El Dorado Resort & Spa

CONTACT:

WEBSITE:
www.eldorado-resort.com

EMAIL:
information@eldorado-resort.com

PHONE:
011-52-998-872-8030

FAX:
011-52-998-872-8034

ADDRESS:
El Dorado Resort
KM. 95 Carretera Nacional
Cancun-Tulum Coast
Quintana Roo, Mexico 77710

authentic Mexican cuisine and La Fontana features Italian cuisine. A reservation is required for dinner at all three on-site restaurants. The resort also has four bars, one swim up bar so you never have to leave the pool and one becomes a disco in the early evening where the party goes all night long.

RATES: Rates are seasonal ranging from $128.00 to $168.00 depending on the suite you choose. Rates are all-inclusive based on single occupancy per person per night.

Emerald Island

The Money Key, Florida

This completely private resort is one of the most exclusive there is. Emerald Island is a magnificent work of art and best of all it is all yours.

Privacy is guaranteed on Emerald Island as only six guests are allowed to stay at once. Yes, it costs a little more, but the privacy and amenities are worth every penny. And best of all, this adult only paradise is also clothing optional. There are no reasons one cannot enjoy a totally uninhibited romp around the estate nude. The only guests are those members in your party.

The rooms are luxuriously large bed and bath suites with a queen bed and private veranda. The master suite offers a spacious king size bed and a whirlpool jacuzzi. The facilities also offer the convenience of a washer and dryer, gourmet kitchen, entertainment center that includes a television, radio and CD player, and a supply of books. The center of attention at the wet bar is the 300 gallon, saltwater aquarium.

Guests of the island may enjoy the use of the 17-foot luxury boat that is included in the stay. Upgrades to a larger 19-foot or 22-foot are available. The island's caretaker will arrange for any needs. Groceries, maid service, chef service, massages, and local excursions are all items that the caretaker can set up for guests upon request.

Relax and bask in the sun, enjoy a fishing trip or cruise around the island in a boat. The decision on what to do is yours. There are no planned events, except the ones you dream of doing.

SERVICES: The caretaker can arrange for groceries, cook, maid, and massages. He can also see to arranging fishing trips, scuba dives, boat trips, sightseeing excursions, and more.

Resorts

Emerald Island

CONTACT:

WEBSITE:
www.privateisland.net

PHONE:
305-745-3084

FAX:
305-745-8843

ADDRESS:
The Money Key, Inc.
516 Caribbean Drive East
Summerland Key, Florida 33042

DINING: Daily meals can be prepared in the gourmet kitchen, with chef services offered upon request and at an additional expense.

RATES: Three large bed and bath suites offer an exclusivity all their own. Rates are seasonal and range from $800.00 nightly with a minimum of a four-night stay to $5500.00 per week.

Located on 18 acres of the most beautiful land in Jamaica, Couples Negril has everything a couple could want in an all-inclusive getaway vacation. Beautiful palms, fragrant floral displays, radiant white sand beaches, and plenty of activities for entertainment are offered.

234 rooms are located at this resort, all with magnificent views. All rooms are equipped with satellite television, hair dryer, air conditioning, CD player, king size bed, private bath, phone, and either a patio or a balcony.

Guests may enjoy fun and frolic in the pool area. With a large pool that spills over into a smaller pool that is equipped with a complete swim-up bar, getting a drink is never an inconvenience. Two jacuzzis, located poolside, are ready to soak away stress and offer relaxation. At this beachside resort, water sports abound. Windsurfing, water skiing, canoeing, and sailing are all wonderful ways to spend the day. Other outdoor activities include volleyball, beach walking, bird watching, and golf. Shopping, glass bottom boat tours, and sunset catamaran cruises are all found near Couples Negril. Indoor activities are also provided and include chess tournaments and billiards.

Three restaurants provide breakfast, lunch, and dinner options. Continental breakfast can be found from 5:00 am to 7:30 am at the Terrace Restaurant with a breakfast buffet served immediately after. Lunch is also offered here as well as a continental al la carte menu for dinner. Mediterranean flavor is the taste of the day at the Beach Grill and the Otaheite Restaurant offers true Caribbean cuisine.

Nighttime brings the entertainment of live bands and dancing the night away.

Weddings may also be accommodated at Couples Negril. Their beautiful wedding gazebo is set near a scenic lily pond. A wondrous setting for nuptials to be exchanged.

Couples Negril is a couple only resort and will not allow any guests younger than 18 years of age. They also have another wonderful retreat located in Negril. "Swept Away Negril" offers an intimate tropical hideaway, wellness retreat and a renowned

10-acre sports complex. Couples Ocho Rios is very similar to Couples Negril, offering many of the same amenities and activities, and is also a couples only retreat.

If you are looking for a tropical paradise, free from children and ready to serve your every need, then give the friendly staff at Couples Resorts a call. They will assist you in choosing the Couples Resort that is right for you and your mate, for your next vacation.

SERVICES: A large pool is available with a smaller pool that offers a swim-up bar. Two jacuzzis for guests' enjoyment are located poolside. Watersports, indoor games, fitness center, golf, bird watching, scuba and volleyball can be found at Couples Negril. The all-inclusive rate covers all meals, snacks, beverages, wine and cocktails, activities, water sports, scuba diving, golf green fees at nearby courses, catamaran cruise, select off-site excursions, airport transfers, taxes and gratuities. Other services, such as massage, are available for a fee.

DINING: Three restaurants offer continental style dining for breakfast, lunch and dinner, and serve Caribbean favorites as well as items with a Mediterranean flavor.

RATES: Rates per couple for a three night stay range from $1550.00 to $2560.00 depending on your accommodations and the time of year.

Couples Negril

CONTACT:

WEBSITE:
www.couples.com

EMAIL:
info@couples.com

PHONE:
800-COUPLES or 305-668-0008

ADDRESS:
Couples Resorts
7775 NW 48th Street
Miami, Florida 33316

Little Palm Island Resort and Spa

Little Torch Key, Florida

This first class resort sits on a small island in the Florida Keys. Twenty-eight bungalows, each housing two bungalow suites, are scattered around the island offering a variety of different views amid luxuriant tropical landscaping. Each secluded, thatched-roof bungalow suite is carefully decorated and provides one bedroom with a king size bed, separate living area, private bath with whirlpool bathtub, and a private terrace. Guests will also find a hair dryer, iron, robes, mini bar, coffee maker, private safe, and data line in each of these suites.

For an even more exclusive experience, try one of the two available Island Grand suites. These, the newest accommodations on the island, offer guests unforgettable luxury with over 900 square feet decorated with fine British Colonial furnishings, including a four-poster bed with romantic netting to set the mood for a memorable evening. These suites also offer slate floors, exquisite chandeliers, his and her bathrooms, an outdoor hot tub, and both indoor and outdoor lounging areas.

If you can pull yourself away from your luxurious accommodations, you'll want to take advantage of the rest of the resort as well. A lovely beach area is outfitted with comfortable lounge chairs for sunning, a Zen garden beckons guests to visit its tranquil embrace, and a fresh water pool waits with cooling waters to refresh and revive. For active souls, a variety of water sports, such as kayaking and wind surfing, are available, as well as fishing charters, scuba diving, snorkeling, and ecological tours.

Be sure to include a trip to the onsite spa each day. Here you will discover a variety of services designed to soothe your body and mind. Many types of massage, beauty treatments, Yoga, and traditional Indonesia rituals are available to guests for an additional charge. Whatever you need to relax is likely to be found here.

Daily dining at Little Palm Island is a vacation all to itself. Under the direction of Chef Adam Votaw, the restaurant serves three meals a day offering gourmet Floribbean cuisine blending flavors of both Florida and the Caribbean with light Asian and French undertones. Breakfast is available in your room, while lunch and dinner are served in the dining room, which sports an available outdoor terrace. Each Sunday, a sumptuous brunch is served and there are also special meals on most holidays.

SERVICES: Daily rates include unlimited water sports, snorkeling and scuba tours, transfers to and from the island, and a daily paper. Spa services are also available for an additional charge.

DINING: Little Palm Island houses its own ocean front restaurant featuring gourmet cuisine. A full meal plan covering breakfast, lunch, and dinner is available for $135.00 per person per day. Guests are also welcome to dine a la carte.

RATES: Rates vary according to package and time of year. Call or visit their website for current pricing information. Little Palm Island Resort is for adults only 16 and over.

Hedonism II

Negril Beach, Jamaica

If you're an open-minded adult looking for an all-inclusive, island vacation with a relentless party atmosphere, Hedonism II may be just the vacation destination you seek. Known for a freewheeling, anything-goes atmosphere, Hedonism II is a place where you can let your hair down and, in some places, take your clothes off.

The resort has 280 rooms with air conditioning, tile floors, private baths, and mirrored ceilings. Each has either two twin beds or one king size bed. Rooms are available with a view of either the garden or the ocean and almost half the rooms are for guests who wish to remain clothes free for the majority of their vacation. Accommodations are comfortable, but small, as most guests of the resort don't spend much time in their rooms.

All meals are included in your stay, and you'll have a variety of tastes to choose from. The daily breakfast buffet is served in the main restaurant, as are lunch and dinner. At lunch, you can also choose to stay near the beach and grab a bite from one of the beach side grills. Dinner is available at the main restaurant or at one of two other themed restaurants on the premises.

The facility has easy access to two beaches—one nude, one not—a fitness facility, a boutique, a pharmacy, a duty free shop, and available spa services. There are also two large, freshwater swimming pools—one nude, one not—and a variety of available land and water sports. Scuba diving is available for an extra fee. At night the resort springs to hedonistic life with various celebrations such as the infamous toga and pajama parties as well as a large nightly bonfire that begs your primal urges to come alive. Mingle with new friends at one of the five bars on the property or head to the disco to dance the night away.

Hedonism III is the newest resort from the creators of the original wicked vacation. This resort is also in Jamaica, but is a little more upscale than Hedonism II, with available amenities such as swim-up rooms and full suites. But don't worry, they still have all the hedonistic action of the original.

Hedonism II

CONTACT:

WEBSITE:
www.superclubs.com

EMAIL:
info@superclubs.com

PHONE:
877-GO-SUPER

ADDRESS:
Hedonism II
Negril Beach, Jamaica

SERVICES: The resort is all-inclusive and offers a gym with state of the art facilities, as well as a boutique, pharmacy, and duty free shop. For a small fee, guests can also enjoy online access via the Internet booth in the lobby.

DINING: Breakfast, lunch, and dinner are served buffet style in the main dining terrace. For dinner, you can also try something a little different at either Pastafari Restaurant featuring pasta dishes with a Jamaican flare, or choose to go totally Jamaican at the Jamaican Restaurant where you can dine under the stars. During the day, grab a quick bite at one of the beachside grills before diving back into your activities. If your partying continues till midnight, you'll find a midnight buffet to keep you going.

RATES: Rates vary depending on time of year. Call or visit their website for current pricing information. Hedonism II and III are both for adults only. Couples and singles are welcome.

Resorts

Cayo Espanto

Caribbean

Located in the beautiful, turquoise waters of the Caribbean and just minutes from San Pedro lies the exquisite and private adult retreat of Cayo Espanto.

Imagine fly-fishing in these radiant waters and landing the big one! Or maybe you would rather watch them in their underwater homes while snorkeling. For the sightseer, there are daily tours to Belize. With the abundant variety of local birds on nearby islands, bird watching is another relaxing alternative to the norm.

Cayo Espanto offers some of the best food and chefs in the region. Their award winning styles will thrill your taste buds and force another notch to be used on your belt. Does grilled duck with ginger and lime sound appealing? How about smoked chicken with sweet potatoes, topped off with a delicious piece of lime pie? These are just a sample of what awaits you in culinary delights.

Cayo Espanto offers five cabanas for guests with a maximum limit of 14 guests allowed on the island at a time. This allows for the ultimate private vacation. With their quality staff numbers, you are assured complete pampering. As a guest, you are provided your own personal butler. Rooms provide satellite television, large terry robes, a complete CD library, king size beds, and your own key to the snack pantry.

Private pools for each cabana and an ocean view are more benefits to guests of Cayo Espanto. Even better, the entire island may be rented to ensure you enjoy a truly private vacation for two!

SERVICES: Kicking back is easy with your own butler and staff tending to your every need. Activities include swimming, fishing, boating, touring, sunbathing, snorkeling, exploring, bird watching and much more.

DINING: Gourmet meals prepared by award winning chefs and served either in your cabana, in bed, or on your own personal veranda. The snack cabinet is available at all times.

RATES: Rates vary based on time of year and number of guests. Range is from $795.00 to $11000.00. Call for details.

Cayo Espanto

CONTACT:

WEBSITE:
www.aprivateisland.com

EMAIL:
info@aprivateisland.com

PHONE:
011-501-26-2473
888-666-4282 or
910-323-8773 (U.S. Reservations)

FAX:
910-323-4272

ADDRESS:
San Pedro
Belize, Central America

Resorts

ADULTS
Only
TRAVEL

Bed & Breakfasts, Villas and Inns

Casa de la Paz Bayfront Bed and Breakfast

St. Augustine, Florida

Overlooking Matanzas Bay in historic St. Augustine, known as the nations oldest city, Casa de la Paz Bayfront Bed and Breakfast is credited as one of Florida's most romantic inns. The historic Mediterranean-style home host six spacious rooms each with a king or queen sized bed, a private tiled bathroom, telephone, cable television, ceiling fans, a decanter of sherry and are furnished reminiscent of the early 1900's era. Two of the rooms feature your own private jacuzzi. Three of the rooms have a fireplace where you and that special someone can snuggle up and enjoy a glass of wine or maybe something a little more intimate.

Most of the guestrooms offer a great view of the bay, the lighthouse or the lush tropical gardens of the courtyard. The aroma of fresh baked goods usually fills the air and the house features brilliantly finished oak wood floors throughout. The lavish décor helps to set the mood for relaxation as soon as you arrive.

If you're a golf enthusiast, St. Augustine is known to have some of the finest golf courses in Florida. Castillo de San Marcos, the Bridge of Lions, the Lighthouse Museum and the Fountain of Youth are among some of the many other local popular attractions for those that don't make it to the putting green. St. Augustine also has over 43 miles of beautiful warm sandy beaches if you just wanted to relax and work on your tan. Many get up early to experience the thrill of watching the sunrise over the waves of the Atlantic Ocean.

The lush tropical garden and flowing fountains in the private courtyard offer the perfect surroundings for a secluded romantic and intimate wedding. Your host can help you arrange everything from the cake to a romantic carriage. The whole inn is available for rent if you want to make it a group wedding or have your entire family stay with you, up to 25 people.

Casa de la Paz Bayfront B & B

CONTACT:

WEBSITE:
www.casadelapaz.com

EMAIL:
info@casadelapaz.com

PHONE:
800-929-2915 or 904 -829-2915

FAX:
904-824-6269

ADDRESS:
Casa de la Paz Bayfront
Bed and Breakfast
22 Avenida Menendez
Saint Augustine, Florida 32084

SERVICES: Services include several theme romantic packages for couples including several golf packages, an anniversary getaway, a romantic spa weekend and a honeymoon night specialty weekend, most of which include a moonlit horse-drawn carriage ride and a dozen roses to help kindle the passion. Complete spa services are also available for an extra fee.

DINING: Full service breakfast is included in your rate and typically includes fruit filled French toast, fresh fruit, muffins, homemade apple butter and other home baked goodies. There are several other dining choices within walking distance of the property.

RATES: The rates vary from $120.00 to $225.00 per night depending on the room and time of year.

Bed & Breakfasts, Villas and Inns

Fantasy Inn & Wedding Chapel

South Lake Tahoe, California

Romance is in the air, wedding bells will ring, and your fantasy waits at Fantasy Inn & Wedding Chapel. This remarkable inn takes you away from reality and allows you to stay in a fantasy theme room that will highlight your stay.

Perfect for a wedding and honeymoon, Fantasy Inn & Wedding Chapel accommodates their guests in special theme rooms. Each one will delight the senses and set you adrift on a sea of enchantment. Themes differ, but the in-room benefits remain the same and are fit for a king or queen! A whirlpool for two is located in each room. Relax in the silken, swirling water or share a European style shower for two. A gift basket of lotion and bubble bath is provided. Set the mood with specialized lighting and relax on the round king size bed, or wave less waterbed, depending on the room, which is set upon a pedestal of light. Entertainment is just a remote click away with the 27-inch swivel television. Stereo system, DVD, and CD players are also located in each room. Toast your vacation or honeymoon choice with the complimentary bottle of wine.

Special packages provide a host of activities to make your trip a memorable one. Ski packages, snowmobile packages, and fantasy packages all provide different forms of activities. The romantic will not have any trouble being stimulated at Fantasy Inn & Wedding Chapel. If you choose to stay at least five nights, your wedding ceremony will be included in the package cost.

This is the perfect getaway for honeymoons, anniversaries, or just a romantic trip for two! Be sure to plan your next romantic retreat at Fantasy Inn & Wedding Chapel.

SERVICES: Special in-room benefits that include whirlpool for two, shower for two, DVD, and CD player. Local activities include skiing and snowmobiles.

DINING: Continental breakfasts are provided with local restaurant facilities nearby.

RATES: Rates range from $159.00 to $359.00 per night with special packages available. Call for details.

Fantasy Inn & Wedding Chapel

CONTACT:

WEBSITE:
www.fantasy-inn.com

EMAIL:
info@fantasy-inn.com

PHONE:
800-367-7736 or 530-541-4200

ADDRESS:
Fantasy Inn & Wedding Chapel
3696 Lake Tahoe Boulevard
South Lake Tahoe, California 96150

Bed & Breakfasts, Villas and Inns

Westwind Inn

Buckhorn, Ontario, Canada

At Westwind Inn you'll enjoy 60 acres of beautiful, tree-laden land, a pristine, nine-acre pond, and a quarter mile of sandy lakefront beach. Even with such generous grounds, the Westwind Inn is home to only 36 guest rooms, so you can count on finding privacy when you want it. Rooms in the main building offer a fireplace, sitting area, private bath, and color TV. Most have balconies as well. For a more exclusive experience, stay in the Chalet, which offers four luxury rooms all with beautiful views of the lake.

Guests are invited to spend time relaxing in the living area of the main lodge where refreshments are offered daily to guests as they play games, read books, and get to know one another. Also in the main lodge are a hot tub, sauna, and lounge with a 61" TV. Walk outside to enjoy the 40 foot heated swimming pool and outdoor hot tub, or try your luck on Westwind's very own putting green complete with sandpit. Venture past the putting green to explore one of the nature trails on the property. While you're out, be sure to look for one of the romantic hammocks for two tucked around the grounds—perfect for an afternoon nap on a warm, summer day. In winter, the grounds are fun for cross-country skiing or snow shoeing.

Breakfast and dinner are included in the price of your stay and are served in a lovely, antique-laden dining room complete with a large, open fireplace, and a panoramic view of the lake. The cuisine is gourmet with a wide variety of selections available, including vegetarian dishes. Special diets can usually be accommodated with advance notice.

As a guest of Westwind, you'll be given complimentary use of their boats, bicycles, skis, and other equipment. For an extra fee,

CONTACT:

WEBSITE:
www.westwindinn.net

EMAIL:
info@westwindinn.net

PHONE:
800-387-8100 or 705-657-8095

ADDRESS:
Westwind Inn
Box 91 Hwy 36
Buckhorn, Ontario, Canada K0L 1J0

your hosts can direct you to boating trips and fishing excursions as well. Other nearby activities include several full size golf courses, boat cruises, and a zoo. Westwind Inn is a quiet retreat catering primarily to adults over the age of 30.

SERVICES: Limousine service is available to and from the airport for an extra fee. Complimentary canoes, kayaks, rowboats, sailboat, pedal boats, sailboard and bikes are offered to guests. For those wishing to tie the knot, a witness can be provided as well as other wedding arrangements to help make the day memorable.

DINING: Breakfast and dinner are included in the price of your stay, and are served at romantic, candlelit tables. For an extra charge, your hosts will pack you a light lunch to go.

RATES: Rates per person per night are from $130.00 to $265.00 depending on accommodations and time of year. Minimum stays are required at various times throughout the year.

Bed & Breakfasts, Villas and Inns

Anniversary Inn

Salt Lake City, Utah

The Anniversary Inn, Salt Lake City, Utah location, is a popular destination for honeymooners, or for any couple that would like to add a little spark of romance to their relationship. The inn is home to a wide variety of themed rooms and suites designed to ignite the romantic imagination. From rugged to opulent, these rooms will have you and your partner inspired in no time.

With more than thirty rooms to spark your interest, you're bound to find one that is just right for you and your sweetheart. Are you an old-fashioned romantic? Then consider a stay in the Romeo and Juliet suite complete with a pillared balcony, tiled floor and curved stairway, or perhaps a stay in the lovely Rose Garden room, which echoes the delicate beauty of an English garden.

Unlock your passion by staying in one of the more exotic rooms such as the Mysteries of Egypt suite. Inside, you'll almost believe you're in one of the ancient pyramids back in the days of its original splendor. But don't worry, modern amenities including, TV, DVD player, and a jetted tub will keep you in 21st century comfort. If money and power gets your heart beating faster, choose the opulent Presidential suite. This finely appointed room with a three-sided fireplace will have you both shouting, "Hail to the Chief!"

Other room themes include the Log Cabin suite, Lighthouse suite, South Pacific suite, and the Italian Gondola suite. Whatever your tastes, the Anniversary Inn can help you find the room that will turn your passion up to full blaze.

There are four Anniversary Inn locations. Two are located in Salt Lake City, Utah, another in Logan, Utah, and one more in Boise, Idaho. All offer the same type of themed rooms for couples.

SERVICES: Limousine service is available.

DINING: Continental breakfast served daily in each room.

RATES: Rates vary by room and range from $129.00 to $269.00 per room on weekday nights and $149.00 to $269.00 on weekend nights.

Anniversary Inn

CONTACT:

WEBSITE:
www.anniversaryinn.com

EMAIL:
info@anniversaryinn.com

PHONE:
800-324-4152

ADDRESS:
Anniversary Inn
460 South 1000 East
Salt Lake City, Utah 84102

Bed & Breakfasts, Villas and Inns

Berkeley Springs Inn

Berkeley Springs, West Virginia

Berkeley Springs Inn is a stately establishment catering to couples only. The grand colonial style house and lush, wooded grounds provide a luxurious retreat for any romantic pair. All rooms are tastefully decorated to reflect the colonial heritage of the area and come with private tiled baths, satellite TV, VCRs, and outdoor decks. King and queen beds are both available.

Start your day with a sumptuous breakfast in the dining room before taking a walk around the seven acres of manicured grounds. Sitting rooms in the inn afford a comfortable place to relax, read a book, or just play games. Don't forget to take advantage of all the spa services offered right on the premises. Manicures, pedicures, facials, tanning, and more are all offered on site for very reasonable prices. Spa package deals that include the price of a room and individual spa services are also available.

Dinners at the inn are lavish. Crisp white tablecloths are adorned with fine china, crystal, silver, and finished with romantic candlelight and flowers. Guests can admire the international art collection that decorates the walls of the dining room while waiting for the chef to prepare dinner. Meals include five courses and the menu changes daily. A selection of wine and cordials is available, but no beer.

President George Washington, who called the town "Bath", settled the town of Berkeley Springs. It is the country's first spa. Early American settlers all along the eastern coast heard about the naturally flowing mineral spring waters and tourists quickly began coming to the area. Today there are several spa facilities in and around the town providing a variety of services such as aromatherapy, homeopathy and massages. Old country stores, as well as antique and gift shops, provide opportunity for shoppers to explore. There are a variety of services to choose from for a quick lunch. If you prefer an itinerary that takes in more of the outdoors, you can choose from golf, tennis, horseback riding and mountain hiking or biking. Many simply spend the day at Berkeley Springs State Park while others enjoy taking the tour of the nearby Berkeley Castle and Luray Caverns.

SERVICES: The Berkeley Springs Inn has jacuzzis and a swimming pool (in season only) and also offers a variety of spa services including massages, steam treatments, a sauna, hair care treatments, facials and pedicures. A complete video library is also available for those that don't want to venture off property for entertainment. Limousine service is available to and from the airport or any of the local attractions.

DINING: Nightly five course dinners are available at candlelight tables for two. Breakfast is served daily between 9:00am and 10:00am. A large selection of wine is available to accompany your gourmet dinner.

RATES: Rates vary according to the season, call for current prices. Berkley Springs Inn is for couples only and is a smoke free establishment.

Bed & Breakfasts, Villas and Inns

Sybaris Romantic Getaways

Northbrook, Illinois

Recognized by the International Hospitality Rating Bureau as one of the best romantic destinations in the United States, Sybaris offer couples looking for an escape of the daily grind the perfect getaway solution. They offer guests choice of six different suites, each with your own private whirlpool for two, fireplace and romantic lighting. Some of the suites have an in-room 16 or 22-foot swimming pool, a private steam room, waterslide and a streaming waterfall that drops from the second story loft.

Romance is the ultimate goal as none of the suites are equipped with a telephone to disturb you. All suites have a king size bed, a television with VCR, a stereo with CD player, a mini-bar and each guest is provided with a terry robe to make your stay more relaxing. Sybaris has five locations spread across the Northern United States. Check out their website for each locations contact information.

SERVICES: Robes are provided for guests in each room and cleaning services are available if you stay multiple nights.

DINING: Although no onsite dinning services are provided each suite is equipped with mini-bar that has a coffee maker, a microwave and a refrigerator with ice awaiting your arrival. A wide range of restaurants are located near each location.

RATES: Room rates are structured two ways. You can rent any of the suites for an entire afternoon from 12:30 to 4:30. The afternoon rates are from $70.00 to $190.00 depending on the suite you choose. Overnight room rates range from $115.00 to $520.00 per night depending on the suite you choose and the day of the week. Sybaris is a private members club and you must become a member to make a reservation. There are three types of memberships available. Membership rates range from $30.00 to $155.00 per couple per year.

Sybaris Romantic Getaways

CONTACT:

WEBSITE:
www.sybaris.com

E-MAIL:
online request form

PHONE:
847-298-5000

FAX:
847-298-7443

ADDRESS:
Sybaris
3350 Milwaukee Ave
Northbrook, Illinois 60062

Bed & Breakfasts, Villas and Inns

Tankah Villas

Tankah Beach, Mexico

If you're looking for a very private Mexican beach experience, Tankah Villas may be perfect for you. This property is located about one and a half hours from the Cancun airport by car and is far removed from the bustling crowds that circle the mega hotels in the city. The main villa, Tankah Villa, sits just off the beach and offers a king size bed and full size futon, as well as a full kitchen, and fabulous views of the beach and surrounding vegetation. You'll also have daily maid service and the option of a cooking service for a nominal, daily fee. There is a good deal of privacy here in the house and on the beach just outside, so it's a perfect spot for going bare and working on your all-over tan. It's also a very romantic setting.

Upon arrival, you'll be greeted with a cooler full of beer and soft drinks and a basket of fruit. Shed your clothes, if you like, and head to the beach for fabulous snorkeling with spectacular coral reefs. Snorkeling and kayaking off the beach are complimentary. If diving is your passion, you'll be pleased to know that there is a dive shop within walking distance. When you're ready for rejuvenation, your hosts can guide you through Yoga and Reikki classes in your villa or on the beach.

Additional accommodations available include Casa Playa Maya, a more upscale home with two bedrooms and a loft, and Casa Jihae and Casa Kristie, which are housed in the same building and together make a very nice duplex. Nudity is fine at Tankah Villa and Casa Playa Maya, and is fine at Casa Jihae and Casa Kristie as long as a nudist group rents both sides.

For those who may want to venture underwater, Tankah Villas is a snorkeling and diving paradise. A living coral reef is very close by and hosts several species of tropical fish. Xel-Ha snorkeling park is just a few minutes away and offers diving with dolphins. Dos Ojos, also just minutes away, offers cavern and underwater cave diving excursions. Don't worry if you forget to bring your snorkeling gear. A wide variety of snorkeling equipment is available at your disposal and is included in your fee. A scuba shop is walking distance from the villa to rent your scuba gear.

SERVICES: Upon arrival, you'll find a cooler of beer and soft drinks along with a fruit basket. During your stay, you'll have complimentary use of snorkeling equipment and kayaks. Daily maid service is also included.

DINING: Continental breakfast served daily. You can also hire an on-site cook for about $11.00 a day. If you choose to dine out, your hosts can recommend several good restaurants nearby.

RATES: Rates per week for Tanka Villa are from $1200.00 per week from June to September, $1500.00 per week from October through November, and $1750.00 per week from December through May. Rates for the weeks of Christmas and New Year are $3795.00. Per week rates for the other villas are slightly higher.

Bed & Breakfasts, Villas and Inns

Cliff House Bed & Breakfast

Freeland, Washington

Just a short drive from Seattle is a wonderland in waiting. Cliff House, located on Whidbey Island, is nestled in a wooded setting, private and breathtaking.

This adult only getaway is only offered to one couple at a time, so it is truly yours to enjoy. Sit next to a cozy fire and relax to the sounds of the woods and wildlife. The beauty of the master bedroom is complimented by the large featherbed and a wall of windows. Lay back and enjoy the view in the comfort of bed! When you awake from a restful night's sleep, enjoy the complimentary continental breakfast that is provided for the first two mornings of your stay. Other meals may be prepared in the fully equipped kitchen.

After your breakfast, enjoy the surrounding area with a walk along the beaches. You may even see a seal or whale along your way. If you want a little more activity, golf, hiking, festivals, fairs, shops, antiques, wineries, tours, and a harbor cruise are all located nearby. Or, you may choose to just relax in the outside jacuzzi or hammock.

This retreat also offers The Cottage, another adult only accommodation located nearby on the very edge of Puget Sound. Rented out to only one couple at a time, it is a secluded retreat like its' sister facility Cliff House. It is equipped with a cozy fireplace, small kitchen, and queen size bed. Continental breakfast is also offered for the first two days.

Step into the wilderness, peaceful and serene, in the beauty of the Northwest for your next vacation or short trip getaway!

SERVICES: Kitchen facilities are provided. Outside jacuzzi and hammock are available to guests and other local attractions and options are located minutes away.

DINING: Continental breakfast is provided for the first two days. Kitchen facilities offer the ability to cook your own fair. Optional dining facilities located in one of the seaside towns nearby.

Cliff House Bed & Breakfast

CONTACT:

WEBSITE:
www.cliffhouse.net

EMAIL:
wink@whidbey.com

PHONE:
800-450-7142 or 360-331-1566

ADDRESS:
Cliff House Bed & Breakfast
727 Windmill Drive
Freeland, Washington 98249

RATES: Cliff House for one couple at a time (two couples by special arrangement) rents for $450.00 per night or $550.00 per night for two couples. The Cottage rents to one couple at a time for $175.00 per night.

Algonquin Lakeside Inn

Dwight, Ontario, Canada

Algonquin Lakeside Inn is a quiet, woodland retreat that is ideal for nature lovers. You'll stay in either a water front room with a private patio or screened porch, one of the fabulous Anniversary Suites, or the Housekeeping Cottages available with a fireplace and romantic jacuzzi tub. All of the rooms have a king or queen size bed. The inn sits on the shores of lovely Oxtongue Lake and offers fabulous views and soothing quiet.

In accommodating weather, guests are taken on a boat ride for a tour of the area to get familiar with the lake. Complimentary canoes and rowboats are available for your private exploring. Make the short trip to nearby Algonquin Park to enjoy spectacular bird watching opportunities, as well as a chance to see a wide variety of wildlife such as moose, bear and deer. The park offers many hiking trails, each with its own beauty to discover. There is also a visitor's center and museum to browse through. More adventuresome souls can try their luck at nearby Ragged Falls, for a beautiful and exciting experience.

Lazy afternoons and evenings can be enjoyed in the game room and lounge, both with a cozy fireplace. This is a great place to unwind after a day outdoors, and also a great place to swap stories with other guests. For those looking for a little more activity, dog sledding, golf, snowmobiling, cross-country ski trails, steamship rides, biking and the local casino offer plenty to keep you busy.

SERVICES: In good weather, the inn offers its guests a complimentary and informative cruise around Oxtongue Lake. Guests are also invited to use the inn's canoes and rowboat to explore the lake.

Bed & Breakfasts, Villas and Inns

DINING: Guests receive a complimentary continental breakfast each morning, and meal plans are available for the rest of the day. Algonquin Inn specializes in home-style cooking. A lounge and bar with a fireplace are also on-site for those that want a relaxing after dinner drink.

RATES: Rates start at $99.95 per night based on double occupancy with a 3-night stay. Call for details.

Algonquin Lakeside Inn

CONTACT:

WEBSITE:
www.algonquininn.com

EMAIL:
stay@algonquininn.com

PHONE:
800-387-2244 or 705-635-2434

ADDRESS:
Algonquin Lakeside Inn
RR Oxtongue Lake
Dwight, Ontario, Canada

Bed & Breakfasts, Villas and Inns

Carriage House at The Harbor

South Haven, Michigan

This Victorian beauty is located just one block from the sandy beaches of lovely Lake Michigan, a quiet setting that's ideal for a romantic getaway. An impressive three floors afford 11 cozy guest rooms, each with it's own private bath. Each room is uniquely decorated with quaint antiques, Amish furniture, and outfitted with a TV and VCR. Other available room amenities include fireplaces, whirlpool baths, showers, decks, and views of either wooded Stanley Johnson Park or the scenic harbor.

Start your day with an old-fashioned country breakfast enjoyed in the breakfast and dining areas downstairs, before stepping out to discover South Haven where a variety of activities on land and sea can be enjoyed in and around the town. If it's water you want, explore one of the many public beaches, or take a trip to the marina to rent a boat or jet ski. If you want to stay on land, your options include golf, horseback riding, spas, several nearby wineries, and much more. During the winter months, take advantage of the snow and ice with skiing, snowmobiling, ice fishing, and skating.

Shopping lovers will enjoy the many unique shops and produce markets available in South Haven. For a bit of local flavor, stop by one of the area's spectacular blueberry farms and pick your own berries for a nominal fee. If you don't want to get your hands dirty, you can just stroll the grounds and buy prepackaged berries before you leave.

For your evening pleasure, there are a wide variety of restaurants with everything from fresh seafood and steak to burgers and fries. If you're looking for entertainment with dinner, check out the local dinner theatre or book a spot on the nightly dinner cruise out of South Haven.

If you're able to make it back to your room at the Carriage House before dinner, the enticing aromas of hors d'oeuvres made fresh and served daily will greet you.

If you're a wine enthusiast, three of West Michigan's finest wineries are nearby for a tasting tour. For those seeking something a bit more adventurous, you might want to try hiking or biking the 33 mile Kal-Haven Trail. The trail takes you between South Haven and Kalamazoo. South Haven is also home to three local golf courses.

Carriage House at The Harbor

CONTACT:

WEBSITE:
www.carriagehouseharbor.com

PHONE:
269-639-2161

FAX:
269-639-2308

ADDRESS:
Carriage House at The Harbor
118 Woodman
South Haven, Michigan 49090

SERVICES: Meeting and conference facilities are available.

DINING: An old-fashion country style breakfast is served daily at 9:00am in the dining room. A variety of complimentary hors d'oeuvres are available each evening.

RATES: Rates range between $140.00 to $190.00 in winter and $160.00 to $240.00 in summer. A two night minimum stay is required for weekend visits from May through October and a three night minimum stay applies to holidays and other special weekends. Rooms are double occupancy only. No pets allowed.

Bed & Breakfasts, Villas and Inns

Pleasure Point Inn

Santa Cruz, California

After lounging on the warm sand of the beach all day, almost nothing can set the mood for the night like sitting in an eight person hot tub sipping on your favorite beverage and watching the sun set right into the ocean. Retreat to your room where you can relax on your own private patio and listen to the soothing splash of the waves on the beach just a few hundred feet away, or cuddle up in front of the fireplace for something a little more intimate. Looking right over the beach of Monterey Bay, Pleasure Point Inn is the perfect destination if you're looking for something to put the flame back into your romance.

All of the rooms have a single person jacuzzi tub, as well as a digital safe, a refrigerator, a microwave oven, a coffee maker, hardwood floors, a color cable TV with DMX music channels, an alarm clock and a few of the rooms have skylights in the ceiling. A welcome basket full of goodies is also waiting in your room upon your first nights arrival.

If you want to venture away for something to keep you busy, the Santa Cruz Beach Boardwalk is just a short distance away and offers an outdoor amusement park with free admission. And for the wine connoisseurs, there are also several wineries close by that offer a great selection of California wines.

SERVICES: They offer several romantic theme packages for those seeking a great anniversary gift or special weekend away. Everything from complete body massages to dinner reservations to local winery tours are available. They also offer a surfing and kayak package for the sports enthusiast. These packages include surfing lessons, dinner for two, expanded continental breakfast and much more. A wide array of on-site spa services are available for guests.

DINING: A continental breakfast is included in your rate. It is served each morning between 8:00am and 10:00am and includes fresh fruit, bagels, muffins, breads, cereal, yogurt, orange juice, coffee or tea.

RATES: There is a two person per room maximum allowed. The rates vary from $165.00 to $265.00 per night depending on room type.

Pleasure Point Inn

CONTACT:

WEBSITE:
www.pleasurepointinn.com

EMAIL:
inquiries@pleasurepointinn.com

PHONE:
831-469-6161 or 877-557-2567

ADDRESS:
Pleasure Point Inn
2-3665 East Cliff Drive
Santa Cruz, California 95062

Bed & Breakfasts, Villas and Inns

Holden House 1902 Bed & Breakfast Inn

Colorado Springs, Colorado

A true work of love and history, Holden House 1902 Bed & Breakfast Inn is a sight to behold. This Victorian residence was restored and opened as a bed and breakfast in the 1980's. It is furnished with antiques and heirlooms from the owner's ancestral past, and adds a beautiful, homey charm. This feel of home is all the more accented by the two resident felines that roam this historical inn.

The adult only inn has several social areas that are shared by guests. Television may be viewed in the front parlor. Outside this room lays the enjoyment of a breathtaking view from a porch swing.

The rooms are all exquisitely decorated with furnishings of the era. The Independent Suite is no different. It has a luxurious canopy bed that is only over-shadowed by the regal Roman style bathtub for two. Each of the other four suites is just as magnificent in their decors.

Guests are treated to a gourmet breakfast that rivals all others. Fresh fruit, juices, gourmet coffees and teas are accents to the highly popular main breakfast entrees served at the Holden House 1902 Bed & Breakfast.

Many activities and attractions may be found within a

Holden House 1902 Bed & Breakfast Inn

CONTACT:

WEBSITE:
www.holdenhouse.com

EMAIL:
mail@holdenhouse.com

PHONE:
719-471-3980 or 888-565-3980

FAX:
719-471-4740

ADDRESS:
Holden House
1902 Bed & Breakfast Inn
1102 West Pikes Peak Avenue
Colorado Springs, Colorado 80904

short distance of the inn. For those that enjoy the physical thrill of soaring down a pounding river, white water rafting can be found only a few miles away. Horseback riding and nature hiking are also located nearby. History buffs will be able to wet their interests in one of several historical locations, also nearby. Shopping and dining options can be enjoyed by the less adventurous within the town of Colorado Springs.

The Holden House 1902 Bed & Breakfast Inn is truly a historical fantasy come true!

SERVICES: Daily maid service, turn down service, and in-room telephones are the hospitalities shown each and every guest. Other services, such as hiking, white water rafting, and shopping are located nearby.

DINING: Gourmet breakfast is served at the guest's choice of 8:00am or 9:00am. Complimentary refreshments are also offered, including their famous Bottomless Cookie Jar and sparkling water.

RATES: Five suites are available for $120.00 to $140.00, with special seasonal packages offered, including their romantic breakfast in bed. Call for details.

Bed & Breakfasts, Villas and Inns

7 Palms Villa

Anguilla, British West Indies

One of the best-kept secrets of the Caribbean, Anguilla is an exclusive tropical paradise with over 30 dazzling white sand covered beaches. With no direct cruise ship or airport access the island is perfect for those seeking the ultimate private getaway. The 35 square mile island is home to only about 10,000 local inhabitants, and has only a couple of traffic lights. The main attraction of the island is privacy for those who want to do nothing more than relax in the warm sun.

7 Palms Villa, a private inn, offers guests the ultimate luxury in lodging. The spacious resort is perched hillside and houses seven huge guestrooms each with a full view of the ocean. There's a 24x20 swimming pool overlooking clear water, a hammock and a jacuzzi where many guest find themselves relaxing after a hard day at the beach. If you were looking indoors to keep you busy, there is a big screen TV with cable access and a satellite dish. There is also a CD Player with a full music library, board games, a VCR & DVD player with several movie selections as well as a complete book library you can utilize to help pass the time.

The inn is lined with terraces and balcony's hanging off each room where you can take in a spectacular sunrise, enjoy a snack for lunch or relax in the moonlight listening to the soothing sound of the ocean with that special someone. No matter how you choose to spend your day the 7 Palms Villa offers you complete peace and tranquility.

SERVICES: Upon arrival, transportation to and from the airport in St. Martin can be arranged to Anguilla by a 20-minute private boat cruise. Massage services, personal trainer, concierge, maid service, fishing trips, boat tours, personal security guard and scuba excursions can be arranged for an extra fee. And for the golf enthusiast, the island is home to a new Greg Norman golf course.

DINING: While the 7 Palms Villa does not offer elaborate dining choices, you won't go hungry. Anguilla is often referred to as the cuisine capital of the Caribbean. While the island is most widely known for its sumptuous seafood, there are over 70 eateries you can choose from featuring anything from American to Italian. So it won't be hard to find something that pleases your palate.

RATES: At 7 Palms you rent the entire villa. There is a seven night minimum stay and the rates vary from $1750.00 to $5000.00 per day depending on the time of year, number of guests and services provided.

Bed & Breakfasts, Villas and Inns

China Clipper Inn

Ouray, Colorado

The China Clipper Inn is a historic building in the Victorian town of Ouray, Colorado, often described as the "Switzerland of America" because of its setting in the spectacular San Juan Mountains. The grand, three-floor home holds twelve generous guest rooms. Each room is uniquely outfitted and named after famous clipper ships. The *Sea Serpent*, for example, is one of the inn's standard rooms on the first floor. *The Witch of the Waves* is a deluxe room on the second floor with a private deck entrance, hot tub, and bay window. All of the rooms vary in size and amenities, but some of the available extras include hot tubs, decks, and fireplaces. All rooms come with a queen size bed, private bath, satellite TV, and two comfy robes for your enjoyment. Décor throughout the China Clipper Inn is stately, yet comfortable, and reflects the building's Victorian heritage. A full, hot breakfast is served each morning in the dining room. On warm days, breakfast can be enjoyed with a dramatic mountain view outside on the covered porch.

For daily activities in Ouray, you're only limit will be your imagination. In the winter months, make the most of the powder perfect snow and dazzling ice formations with ice-skating, ice climbing, snowboarding, and skiing. As a bonus, the inn offers guests half price lift tickets to nearby Telluride. You can try Ouray's Hot Springs pool any time of year, but during winter, guests of the China Clipper Inn receive half price passes to this natural wonder. Warm weather activities include swimming, fishing, hiking, and mine tours, just to name a few.

For a more leisurely pace, stroll through the many shops and stop by one of Ouray's coffee houses to relax and refresh. For lunch and dinner there are many local restaurants offering a wide variety of food choices from French cuisine to burgers. In the summer months, try an old-fashioned cowboy cookout up in the mountains.

SERVICES: Massages can be arranged by appointment.

DINING: Full breakfast and afternoon beverages are served daily.

China Clipper Inn

CONTACT:

WEBSITE:
www.chinaclipperinn.com

EMAIL:
china5@mindspring.com

PHONE:
800-315-0565 or 970-325-0565

FAX:
970-325-4190

ADDRESS:
China Clipper Inn
525 Second Street
Ouray, Colorado 81427

RATES: Nightly rates are $75.00 to $170.00 during the winter and $100.00 to $170.00 in the summer. Most holiday nights are priced at summer rates and may require a two-night minimum stay. The inn is non-smoking and for adult couples only. No pets are allowed.

Bed & Breakfasts, Villas and Inns

Felton Crest Inn

Felton, California

Nestled between huge redwoods in the mountains on a private road, Felton Crest Inn is an exclusive romantic getaway that offer guests the right ingredients for an ultimate weekend away. If you enjoy the peace and tranquility of the woods, this destination will prove to be an escape from reality with many trails deep into the forest.

The inn is located just minutes from Big Basin Redwoods State Park and Henry Cowell Redwoods State Park, which are quite popular to visit. The area is known for great wine. There are over forty local wineries surrounding the Felton, many of which offer tasting and facility tours. All of them have their own unique blends so you'll be sure to find something that pleases your palate.

There are four rooms all with an excellent view of the surrounding forest. The Tree Top Penthouse suite is the most luxurious of the four. The room has vaulted ceilings, stained glass windows, a California king sized bed, ceiling fan, fireplace, big screen TV with VCR, DVD player with 45 movie selections and a private deck that opens into the woods, just to name a few of the amenities this room offers. All of the rooms have a private bathroom with a full jacuzzi or add-on whirlpool bath, a television with VCR and video library and a telephone. But no matter which room you end up in, each has a bottle of champagne and chocolate kisses that will be awaiting your arrival.

SERVICES: A full continental breakfast is served. If you want a break from your room, the Inn offers use of a furnished plush living area with a fireplace where you can enjoy the conversation of other guests and your host.

DINING: Continental breakfast is included in your rate. A wide variety of cuisine choices are available within minutes of the Inn and vary from German, Italian and Mexican choices. If you're in the mood for something a little more festive, you can order a picnic lunch from one of the local delicatessens that you can enjoy on the beach or at one of the local parks.

RATES: The rates vary from $215.00 to $325.00 per night depending on the room type.

Felton Crest Inn

CONTACT:

WEBSITE:
www.feltoncrest.com

E-MAIL:
hannapeters@mymailstation.com

PHONE:
831-335-4011 or 800-474-4011

ADDRESS:
Felton Crest Inn
780 El Solyo Heights Drive
Felton, California 95018

Bed & Breakfasts, Villas and Inns

Hunter Creek Inn

Minden, Ontario, Canada

This is a true country getaway to relish. Hunter Creek Inn is located next to Gull River in beautiful Ontario, Canada. The inn is a lavish affair with simple pleasures. Guests of the inn will enjoy the peaceful surroundings of the river and country setting.

There is nothing simple about the accommodations! Wonderfully decorated rooms are equipped with various amenities, depending upon the room chosen. Color television, refrigerator, bar, balconies, decks, kitchenettes, queen, double and sofa beds, single and double whirlpools, and private baths are just a taste of what awaits guests of Hunter Creek Inn.

Speaking of taste, Hunter Creek Inn serves delicious, home cooked meals. Guests are allowed to bring their own wine for dinner, or alcoholic beverages to the party room. Other dining options are available nearby, with a wide selection to choose from.

Daily activities, depending on the season, for those that just cannot sit still, include fishing, boating, swimming, canoeing, and paddleboats. There is even a fire pit for barbecues. Wintertime activities are cross-country skiing, skating, ice racing, toboggans, and sleds. Nearby guests can find tennis, ice fishing, shopping, snowmobiles, and much more.

Although this country inn is for couples only, there is plenty to see and do on your vacation getaway. Best of all, you can do it together! Try the Hunter Creek Inn for your next retreat!

SERVICES: Numerous services are provided at Hunter Creek Inn including boating, swimming, sauna, whirlpool, in-room whirlpools in select rooms, fishing, skiing, skating, sleds, and much more.

DINING: Wonderful home cooked meals are offered and guests may bring their own wine and other spirits to the dining room or party room.

RATES: All-inclusive rates are based on days of week and are set up per person per night. The range is $69.00 to $249.00 per night or $399.00 to $1499.00 per week. Accommodation only packages are also available. This is an adult couples romantic destination.

Hunter Creek Inn

CONTACT:

WEBSITE:
www.huntercreekinn.com

E-MAIL:
info@huntercreekinn.com

PHONE:
705-286-3194

ADDRESS:
Hunter Creek Inn
P.O. Box 765
Minden, Ontario, Canada K0M 2K0

Bed & Breakfasts, Villas and Inns

Evening Shade Inn

Eureka Springs, Arkansas

Deep within the Ozark Mountains, lies a secret. That secret is one of the most beautiful, adult only retreats available . . . Evening Shade Inn. Antiques and Lace, the bed and breakfast inn located at Evening Shade Inn has rooms that will set their guests in the lap of luxury. With the jacuzzi for two, king size bed and evening champagne, a couple will fall in love all over again. Rooms are also equipped with private baths, phones with voice mail, cable TV, HBO, VCR, free movies, and coffeemaker. Breakfast is served in your room anytime you wish. They even leave an evening snack. There is also a Honeymoon Suite that has all the benefits of the regular rooms, however it has the added benefit of a fireplace, refrigerator, and microwave.

If more privacy is desired, then a stay in the lovely Honeymoon Cottage or the Antiques and Lace Honeymoon Cottage. Both offer all the amenities of the rooms and suite, plus there is a private balcony or deck, depending on which cottage you choose.

Entertainment can be found within Eureka Springs. There are many outstanding and quaint little shops to while away the days. Many local festivals, shows, and fairs may be enjoyed as well. With the beauty of the area, guests may wish to take a long, romantic walk in the woods and take in the majesty of the Ozark Mountains. Couples wanting to get married may plan their small, intimate wedding without guests, at Evening Shade Inn for only $100.00. What a wonderful prospect for any lucky couple!

SERVICES: Local events, stores, and festivals may be found within Eureka Springs.

DINING: Breakfast is served daily, and at any desired time, privately within rooms or cottages. An evening snack is also provided. You may find other meal options available at restaurants located in Eureka Springs.

RATES: Rooms are $120.00 per night, with the Honeymoon Suite at $135.00 per night. Cottages are $140.00 to $160.00 per night depending on which cottage is desired.

Evening Shade Inn

CONTACT:

WEBSITE:
www.eveningshade.com

EMAIL:
evening@ipa.net

PHONE:
479-253-6264 or 888-992-1224

ADDRESS:
Evening Shade Inn
Hwy 62 East
3079 East Van Buren
Eureka Springs, Arkansas 72632

Bed & Breakfasts, Villas and Inns

Hale Akua Shangri-La

Bed & Breakfast Retreat Center,
Maui, Hawaii

Private, magnificent, and spiritual are the only words that can describe Hale Akua Shangri-La. This clothing optional retreat center is a bed and breakfast that will never be forgotten. It is the complete retreat! From its Grand View Suite to the Poolside Room, every inch of the fabulous center is blessed with scenery to peak the inner soul. These rooms share kitchen and dining facilities, allowing for social interaction when desired. In most cases, showers are outdoors allowing for a naturalistic atmosphere.

Guests may partake in a number of activities that are both healing and meaningful. Yoga, massage therapy, nature and healing walks, and horseback riding adventures give physical and mental healing and entertainment. To soothe the inner soul, guests can have astrology readings. For those with the desire to stimulate or enhance their sexual lives, Oceanic Tantra, a specially designed art of sexual stimulation, is offered. All of these unique services are performed and supervised by professionals in their respective fields.

A hot tub is available for a steamy and relaxing soak that will soothe both the body and the soul. A regular calendar of events that highlight their wide array of services is also offered. Guests may also choose to sit back and soak in the wondrous beauty and climate that only Hawaii can provide!

Hale Akua Shangri-La also has the means to provide services and accommodations for workshops at special rates, with a local caterer available to provide meals.

This is the perfect place to sit back and find the true person within!

SERVICES: Guests may enjoy the hot tub, Yoga, massage therapy, acupuncture, nature walks, horseback riding adventures, astrology, and sexual healing.

DINING: Shared kitchen and dining facilities allow for meals to be prepared and enjoyed. Catering is also available for large groups.

RATES: 13 rooms ranging in prices of $60.00 a day or $378.00 a week for the poolside room to $165.00 a day or $1043.00 a week for the Grand View Suite.

Hale Akua Shangri-La

CONTACT:

WEBSITE:
www.haleakua.com

EMAIL:
reservations@haleakua.com

PHONE:
888-368-5305 (U.S. & Canada)
808-572-9300
(Within Hawaii or outside the U.S.)

FAX:
808-572-6666

ADDRESS:
Hale Akua Shangri-La
Star Route 1, Box 161
Haiku, Maui, Hawaii 96708

Bed & Breakfasts, Villas and Inns

Playa Naturel

Tankah, Mexico

Playa Naturel is located on the Yucatan Peninsula of Mexico near Tulum, 70 miles south of Cancun airport on Tankah Bay. The property is adults only, open to both singles and couples and has a private nude beach overlooking the Caribbean where you can lounge away the days in paradise. If you're ready to enjoy a more natural setting you'll love their four, two story thatched roof palapas that accommodate a maximum of 14 guests. This cozy retreat offers personal yoga sessions as well as individual or group instruction. Your privacy and security are ensured with a stonewall that encircles the property.

Whether you're an experienced snorkeler or are ready to learn, Playa Naturel offers beautiful waters protected by reef for your exploration. This wonderful little property is the perfect spot for a real laid back and naturel vacation, a romantic getaway, or a group adventure with friends. Don't expect the many amenities of a large resort or you will be disappointed. While there is no shortage of activities to keep you busy including tours to the Mayan Ruins and the Sian Kaan Biosphere Reserve, Playa Naturel is more about getting away from it all; unwinding, shedding your clothes and enjoying being in a much more relaxed environment.

SERVICES: Private nude beach and lots of personal attention. Snorkeling, sea kayaks and other water sports available as well as instruction. Ceiling fans and a nice breeze replace air-conditioning in the rooms. Beer, wine and other bar drinks available for an additional charge.

DINING: Breakfast is included with the room price. For an extra fee the staff will prepare lunch and dinner from a local selection of favorites including some great seafood. There are also some very good local restaurants in the area.

RATES: Seasonal rates range from $125.00 to $175.00 per couple per night. There is also an all-inclusive rate available which includes three meals per day as well as beer and wine. You have your choice of the four different bungalows. One large bungalow is available that sleeps two couples. Check in/out times are very flexible. There is no air-conditioning, TV, radio or public phones.

Playa Naturel

CONTACT:

WEBSITE:
www.playanaturel.com

EMAIL:
reservations@playanaturel.com

PHONE:
888-729-0771 or 770-536-8095

FAX:
770-536-6446

ADDRESS:
Playa Naturel
Tankah, Mexico

Bed & Breakfasts, Villas and Inns

Casa Tiene Vista

Sedona, Arizona

asa Tiene means "House with a view". Privately situated on a one-acre hilltop with a beautiful view of the famous Sedona "Red Rocks", Casa Tiene Vista offers couples a unique clothing optional romantic experience. Casa Tiene only accepts one couple at a time. Once you arrive you have full use of the very private pool and spa as well as the freedom to be completely nude your entire stay. Nudity is fully accepted anywhere on the property and according to the owners; you're welcome to be nude from the time you arrive until you depart.

Your accommodations consist of a very intimately designed room with rustic furniture and accessories and a fantastic view from every window. You will really enjoy your own private patio that is adjacent to your own pool and spa. The private spa makes for the perfect place to enjoy a nice romantic evening, complete with bottle of wine and the awesome view of the night sky over Sedona. Casa Tiene also offers a fantastic outdoor fireplace to cozy up next to. And if all of this is not enough to totally relax you, they also offer massage services that you can enjoy poolside while drifting off into another world.

Avail yourself of the heated, indoor swimming pool, sauna, and hot tub, or for more extensive pampering, head to the onsite spa. At the spa, an extensive variety of massage and beauty treatments, as well as other healing therapies are available for an extra charge. There are also spa packages offering discounts on spa bundled services.

A stay at Casa Tiene is all about total relaxation in an environment that lets you be yourself, enjoy the beauty and do it au natarel. If you enjoy the utmost in personal pampering, the freedom to shed your clothes if you desire, and a superb attention to detail, then consider a stay at this private paradise.

Casa Tiene Vista

CONTACT:

WEBSITE:
www.casatienevista.net

EMAIL:
casatienevista.net@earthlink.net

PHONE:
928-274-2230

ADDRESS:
Casa Tiene Vista
Sedona, Arizona

SERVICES: Private spa, pool and outdoor fireplace as well as massage services on the property. Full nudity during your entire stay is acceptable.

DINING: Breakfast is included in the price of your stay and can be served poolside or in the privacy of your room. Bottled water, coffee, tea and ice are also provided in your room.

RATES: Room rate is $210.00 per night and is for one couple. Only one couple can stay at Casa Tiene and a two night minimum stay is required. No pets or smoking allowed. Adult couples only.

Guest House Log Cottages

Greenbank, Washington

Privacy, peace, and beauty are the main attractions at the Guest House Log Cottages. Located on 25 acres, just a little more than an hour's drive from Seattle, Washington, Guest House offers a wide variety of in-cottage benefits.

Private, personal jacuzzi's, kitchens, fireplaces, TV/VCR's with 500 free movies, and an individual setting compliment each cottage Guest House. The Lodge reflects romantically off the still pond. Behind its doors lies enough luxury to soothe the beast in anyone. Guests can wash away their cares and woes in the jetted tub or jacuzzi below a glass ceiling. Afterwards, the king size bed offers even the worst insomniacs the promise of a peaceful night's rest. While the Guest House does not stipulate adults only, they do ask that no children older than four months old accompany guests, which pretty much assures you of an adult atmosphere to enjoy.

All guests are allowed the use of the outdoor swimming pool, hot tub, and exercise room. Breakfast foods are supplied for the first two days of the stay. Other meals may be prepared within the cottages' private kitchens.

SERVICES: Guests are able to enjoy the outdoor pool, hot tub, and exercise room.

DINING: For the first two days, breakfast is included with the stay. The table in the cottage is set, and breakfast foods are placed in the refrigerator, allowing guests to enjoy a meal in whatever state of dress they choose.

RATES: Cottages range from $165.00 to $210.00 per night and the luxury of the Lodge may be enjoyed for $325.00 per night, with a minimum of a two-night stay.

Bed & Breakfasts, Villas and Inns

Garden of Eden Bed & Breakfast

Mazatlan, Mexico

Tranquility and comfort can be found at Garden of Eden Bed and Breakfast in beautiful Mazatlan, Mexico. Renowned for its popularity, Mazatlan is a tourist's paradise. Just a few, short blocks away, guests of the Garden of Eden can enjoy viewing the breathtaking plummet of cliff divers or relax at an intimate dinner at one of the local restaurants that offer a picturesque view of the ocean. Patrons of the arts will enjoy a visit to the Angela Peralta Theater.

Back at the Garden of Eden, you will be able to completely relax within the quiet and serene rooms and gardens. The adult only rule allows for complete peace to enjoy uninterrupted reading, writing, or bird watching. The sounds emanating from the fountain and birds are natural stress reducers. If you are looking for a home away from home, Garden of Eden is the one to choose.

Garden of Eden Bed & Breakfast

CONTACT:

WEBSITE:
www.gardenofeden.com.mx

EMAIL:
gardenofeden@mazatlan.com.mx

PHONE:
011-52-669-982-59-71

ADDRESS:
Garden of Eden
V. Carranza 68 Sur.
Olas Altas
Mazatlan, Mexico

SERVICES: Few services are available at the Garden of Eden, however many attractions are located within a few blocks.

DINING: A wide variety of breakfast foods are offered daily between 7:00am and 10:00am, with alternative dining options available a short two blocks away.

RATES: Smoking and non-smoking rooms are available. A one-bedroom for one to two people is $600.00 pesos ($55.05 USD) or two people in a two-bedroom cost $750.00 pesos ($68.82 USD). An additional person may be added for a cost of $200.00 pesos ($18.35 USD).

Relax. Sleep. Breath. Get away from the noise, the lights, and the people. Visit this charming diminutive cottage and enjoy a truly simple escape. This inviting wooden structure sitting on a lovely half acre provides an intimate retreat for couples looking to renew and refresh. As such, it's a popular choice for anniversary getaways. The cottage has one bedroom, a spacious bathroom with spa tub and steam shower, a fully stocked kitchen, and a cozy living area with fireplace. All the rooms are thoughtfully decorated with soothing colors and textures to enhance relaxation. Sit on the welcoming front porch and watch the dappled light trickle through the tall trees, or sit out back and enjoy the lush green of the large lawn. Be on the lookout for area wildlife including a family of deer that often wander past the cottage. Winter days offer the perfect excuse to simply curl up by the fire with that book you've wanted to read for months.

Start your morning with something from the breakfast basket delivered to your door. This continental meal is just right for most, but special diets can also be accommodated if you inquire ahead.

Daily activities in the area include biking, hiking, and kayaking. A simple drive around the vicinity is fun for those who like to explore. Magnificent homes and views abound, so bring your camera. Stop by the general store in town for some ice cream and a chat with the locals. If you're an art connoisseur, check out the area's two art galleries. During your stay, lunch and dinner can be enjoyed out at one of the bay's many coastal restaurants. If you're a cook, gather fresh seafood ingredients at a dockside market and make use of the cottage's kitchen.

The cottage at Simple Escapes is strictly for those wanting to relax and unwind. If you're a thrill seeker, or if you can't live

Bed & Breakfasts, Villas and Inns

153

without a TV, it may not be for you. If you are looking for tranquility, this is an excellent choice.

SERVICES: Massage services can be arranged onsite for $75.00 an hour.

DINING: Complimentary continental-style breakfasts are provided each morning. A fully stocked kitchen is available for use in the cottage.

RATES: Rates average $129.00 per night in winter to $149.00 per night in summer. Adults only.

Simple Escapes Retreat

CONTACT:

WEBSITE:
www.simplescapes.com

EMAIL:
makeyourescape@simplescapes.com

PHONE:
604-885-9604

ADDRESS:
Simple Escapes Retreat
7784 Lohn Road
Halfmoon Bay, British Columbia,
Canada V0N 1Y0

Morningside Inn

Palm Springs, California

A naturalist's true paradise, Morningside Inn in Palm Springs, California is a secure, clothing optional retreat. Relaxation is easily found amid the swaying palm trees and floral settings of the courtyard. The poolside area offers a refreshing misting system to cool off even the hottest guest.

Seven suites and three rooms make up this adult only bed and breakfast. Guests are offered the comforts of in-room refrigerators, microwaves, phones, cable television with VCR and use of the extensive library of video movies. The suites also are equipped with full kitchens. Massage services, an outdoor gift shop, and free airport pick-up/drop-off is available. A delicious continental breakfast buffet is served daily and an offering of afternoon snacks, wine, and sweet tray is provided. Lunches are provided on the weekends.

Palm Springs offers some of the best vacation attractions in California. The Palm Springs Tram is a favorite in the summer.

Bed & Breakfasts, Villas and Inns

155

CONTACT:

WEBSITE:
www.morningsideinn.com

EMAIL:
jill@morningsideinn.com

PHONE:
760-325-2668 or 800-916-2668

The tram ascends more than 8000 feet to the top of the Smokey Mountains where it is 40 degrees cooler. Other local attractions include shopping, dining, hiking, more than one hundred art galleries to visit, Joshua Tree National Park, over a hundred golf courses and sightseeing just to mention a few of the things to indulge in.

After a hard day of taking in all the local sites most people find themselves poolside to enjoy the breathtaking sunset into the San Jacinto Mountains.

Be sure to check out this unique blend of beauty and freedom when you are planning your next vacation. If you want to relieve yourself from all of the confines of society, then give Morningside Inn a try. You'll be glad you did!

SERVICES: Beautiful, relaxing settings include a private courtyard, pool, outdoor misting system, a gift shop, massage services, maid service and airport pickup/drop-off. Local attractions include shops, restaurants, museums, hiking and sightseeing.

DINING: Daily continental breakfasts are served, buffet style, with afternoon snacks, wine, and sweet tray also provided. Lunches are also provided on Saturdays and Sundays.

RATES: Rates are based on the day of the week and range from $95.00 to $135.00 nightly or $606.00 to $755.00 weekly. Address and directions will be provided by telephone or email after reservations are made.

SeaHorse Inn

The beauty of the tropical Caribbean is the backdrop for this secluded, paradise vacation destination. Accessible only by ferry, SeaHorse Inn offers a wide variety of activities accented by simple, but cozy accommodations.

Rooms offer a television and phone free environment to eliminate outside interference of your relaxing vacation. Because of the constant tropical island breezes, air conditioning is not needed. The five rooms have private bath and showers, bottled water and a few offer guests an in-room refrigerator.

Local activities include snorkeling and diving. A pool is also available. Breakfast is served daily with lunch prepared upon request. Other dining facilities may be found nearby and within walking distance of the inn. Arrangements can be made for horseback riding, nature walks, and car rentals for those that would like to explore St. Lucia by car. However, one must be familiar with, or ready to take on, left-handed driving, the method used on St. Lucia.

Relax in the common room and enjoy one of the books from the library, or take a leisurely stroll through the garden.

Let the lull of this tropical retreat take you away from the worry and stress of everyday life, and soak up the wonderful sunlight. Rejuvenate yourself and your romance at SeaHorse Inn, in beautiful St. Lucia, West Indies.

SERVICES: Pool available for guest use. Touring, snorkeling, diving, horseback riding, hiking, and nature walks can be arranged upon request by the staff.

Bed & Breakfasts, Villas and Inns

SeaHorse Inn

CONTACT:

WEBSITE:
www.seahorse-inn.com

EMAIL:
info@seahorse-inn.com

PHONE:
758-451-4436

FAX:
758-451-4872

ADDRESS:
SeaHorse Inn
P.O. Box 1825, Castries
St. Lucia, West Indies

DINING: Breakfast is served daily and lunch will be prepared upon request. Local dining facilities are located within walking distance of the inn.

RATES: Five rooms are available with an array of seasonal rates ranging from $860.00 per week May through October to $930.00 per week November through April. During the period of December 25 through January 2 an additional $70.00 fee will be charged per week. Children over the age of 14 are permitted.

The beauty and splendor of Canada awaits visitors, but this hotel wonder will not be ready until winter. Ice Hotel is a structure completely constructed of glacier ice and snow. Not just a snowman piece of art, this is a fully functional hotel with wonderful accommodations.

Imagine a romantic night completely engulfed in a room of ice, snuggled down with the one you love, under a cozy pile of deer pelts. Furnishings at this hotel are also lavishly and lovingly sculpted of ice.

The ice bar is fully functional and ready to serve thirsty guests. This is a perfect party place for that special occasion. The art galleries display ice sculptures created by the workers that designed and sculpted the Ice Hotel.

The heartbreaker of this location is it will melt away in the warmth of springtime. But, come each winter, the structure is

Bed & Breakfasts, Villas and Inns

once again rebuilt. The loving dedication of the designers and sculptors has made this an attraction that hundreds of visitors flock to each season. If you would rather not stay in the hotel accommodations, you must at least visit it, and take a tour. Daily visits are accommodated and cost a nominal fee.

Take in the beauty of Canada on your next vacation and travel to the Ice Hotel. The newest hotel around, every year!

RATES: Room rates average $200.00 (CAN) per person, per night, based on double occupancy. Discounts on shared accommodations. Special adventure and wedding packages are available.

Cape May, New Jersey

The Southern Mansion in Cape May, New Jersey is a true historical monument. Restored in the 1990's, this wonderful bed and breakfast lets its guests roam back to a time of horse and buggies and ladies sporting only the finest frills and hoop skirt dresses. Its grand appearance gives way to historical fantasy. Accommodating adults only, Southern Mansion offers only the best and most exquisite furnishings available.

The beautifully elegant rooms feature antique furniture, hair dryers, makeup/shaving mirrors, cable television, individual climate control, maid, and turndown service, and most provide the guest with a king size bed. The elegant Main Mansion offers up to 14 guest rooms and can easily provide for up to 30 guests.

Southern Mansion offers several wedding packages from a small intimate wedding to a lavish affair that costs up to $85.00 per person, providing only the finest cuisine available. If you are looking for the perfect setting for your wedding and honeymoon, then call the hosts of Southern Mansion to start planning the happy event.

Guests may while away their days among the beautiful gardens, or set out on one of the many day trips that Southern Mansion has to offer. Many of these trips include a meal in the package price and offer a variety of sightseeing adventures. Guests may also choose from a variety of activities that include whale watching, kayaking, windsurfing, sailing, bicycling, bird watching, and carriage tours.

Elegant meals are available in the solarium, at an additional cost, and offer only the best foods and desserts. Breakfast is served daily in the solarium. Other offerings, at additional cost, are roses, chocolates, fruit baskets, and cheese and fruit plates.

Bed & Breakfasts, Villas and Inns

Other meal options are offered at one of the many local restaurants. Fine dining, seafood and Italian foods are just some of the types of dining facilities available, and located a short distance from Southern Mansion. Try an intimate dinner for two at one of these many businesses and you will not be disappointed!

Even the most discriminating romantic will be satisfied with a stay at Southern Mansion. A romantic retreat for those that want to be enchanted by the feel of days gone by!

SERVICES: Sightseeing tours with some meals included are an offering of Southern Mansion. Other activities may be arranged and include carriage tours, kayaking, bird watching, whale watching and a variety of water sports. In-room massage services can be arranged for an extra fee. If you were looking to surprise that special someone, arrangements can be made to have a dozen roses, fresh made chocolate covered strawberries, a cheese and fruit platter or a variety of other goodies awaiting both your arrival.

DINING: Breakfast is served daily in the solarium. Evening meals may also be enjoyed in the solarium at an additional cost. Local restaurants provide a wide variety of meal options and types of cuisine.

RATES: Up to 14 guest rooms provide for up to 30 guests. Rates vary depending on time of year, days of week, and room desired. Special packages are available. Call for details and prices.

Post Ranch Inn

Big Sur, California

Amid the radiant mountains and along the misty coast of Big Sur, California is the Post Ranch Inn. Guests receive a natural, peaceful and magnificent atmosphere here.

Rooms are set among some of the most beautiful and breathtaking views available in California. Scenic views of crested mountains, tree-thickened forests and salty shorelines beg your appreciation. The décor lends to the natural feel, with strong use of wood and earthy tones. One group of rooms is enclosed in a tree house, adding to the blend with nature. Each of the 30 rooms is equipped with a king size bed, refrigerator filled with snacks and non-alcoholic beverages, in-room spa tub, collapsible massage table, bathrobes, hair dryer, fireplace, and coffee maker. Television is not a luxury at Post Ranch Inn. It is an interference of the peaceful surroundings. Therefore, there are no TV's provided in the rooms. Music may be enjoyed with an in-room CD player, cassette stereo system and a DMX satellite music system.

Guests may enjoy long scenic walks along the beach, mountain drives, or nature hiking. Lighthouse tours offer a romance all their own. Riding horse back along majestic forests or taking a mountain bicycle ride will strengthen guests' oneness with nature and each other.

Dining is an adventure all its own. Continental breakfasts are served daily and lunches are light and offer both restaurant dining or picnic basket meals. Dinner is the event of the day. With award winning choices, the four-course meal provides a bountiful feast. Their unique options allow guests to indulge in the unknown. Chilled Diamond Oysters, Cured Salmon Napoleon and Veal Paillard with Swiss Chard are just a few of the entrée options prepared by the professional chefs in the kitchens of Post Ranch Inn.

Post Ranch Inn

CONTACT:

WEBSITE:
www.postranchinn.com

EMAIL:
res@postranchinn.com
(Reservations)
info@postranchinn.com
(Information)

PHONE:
800-527-2200 (Reservations)
831-667-2200 (Information)

FAX:
831-667-2824

ADDRESS:
Post Ranch Inn
Highway 1, P.O. Box 219
Big Sur, California 93920

For a romantic getaway, with no children, get back to nature at the Post Ranch Inn. A peaceful, serene vacation for the nature lover in everyone!

SERVICES: Post Ranch Inn has activities based around their mountain setting. Swimming pool, spa services provide massages, facials and a basking pool, hiking, exploring, lighthouse tours, beach walks, bicycling, and horseback riding are further activity options.

DINING: The Sierra Mar Restaurant provides a continental breakfast daily. Lunches range from a picnic basket lunch to light lunches in the restaurant. Dinners are elaborate affairs with a fixed menu that changes daily. A la carte options are available to guests, as well.

RATES: 30 Rooms are available. Guests must be 18 years of age or older to stay. Call or email for detailed rates.

The Sea Garden is a peaceful retreat with spa amenities located on Canada's breathtaking western coast. Here you will find an extremely private sanctuary, far from the stresses of everyday life. Once you check in, you'll find that your room has generous ocean views, a deck and sitting room, and a private bathroom with a large hot tub for soaking and relaxing in. Queen size beds are outfitted with comfortable, high-quality linens and there are robes ready for you to snuggle up in.

The property offers access to a secluded beach, perfect for beachcombing and silent meditation, or just for watching the waves roll up the sand. Be sure to try the onsite spa room, complete with hot tub, sauna, and shower. This room of cedar walls and tile floors is also called the Tree Room for its abundance of decorative trees and plants. There is also a small area with a table and chairs that's ideal for playing games or sipping a beverage in the afternoon.

A specialty of the retreat is Polarity Therapy and massage. Polarity Therapy is an energy-based therapy that involves the body, diet, exercise, and mind. The owner of the facility is trained in this discipline and private sessions and instruction are available for both two-day retreats and day spas. Call to inquire about special package deals incorporating this feature.

Breakfasts are served daily and feature organic ingredients wherever possible. A typical breakfast might include organic, range-free eggs, homemade granola with cashews, muffins, fresh fruit, coffee, and juice. Special dietary needs can be accommodated with advance notice. For lunch and dinner, you're on your own to sample some of the many restaurants along the coast. As you might expect, there are many restaurants specializing in local seafood delicacies, but a variety of cuisine is available.

Bed & Breakfasts, Villas and Inns

Sea Garden Retreat

CONTACT:

WEBSITE:
www.seagardenretreat.com

EMAIL:
info@seagardenretreat.com

PHONE:
866-886-4643 or 604-886-4643

FAX:
604-886-4619

ADDRESS:
Sea Garden Retreat
Gibsons, British Columbia, Canada

SERVICES: Available services include massage, Polarity Therapy, and Polarity mini courses.

DINING: Breakfasts are served daily and consist of mainly organic products.

RATES: Rates average $115.00 to $135.00 per night. Two nights minimum stay is required. Many packages available including a day spa package. Check website for current rates and available packages.

Hotel Makanda by the Sea

Manuel Antonio, Costa Rica

Set between the coast of the majestic Pacific and the dense, green jungle of Costa Rica, Hotel Makanda is both an exotic, ecological experience and a luxurious vacation spot. The original building was built to be a home, and was constructed with a contemporary design to blend comfortably into its natural setting on the hillside above the ocean. Today, all the buildings at Hotel Makanda reflect this original intent. The buildings are open and airy and all have spectacular views of the wild and rugged waves below. For guests' enjoyment, a unique freshwater pool surrounded by over four thousand feet of space for sunning and relaxing is set on the hillside.

Guest rooms are comfortably appointed with vaulted ceilings, king size beds, unique tiling, and carefully chosen furniture. Patios, balconies, full kitchens, private baths, and Japanese gardens make the accommodations both luxurious and convenient. Each day, begin your adventures indulging in a complimentary breakfast with a tropical flare. Then listen as rainforests to the east and coastline to the west beckon you outdoors to explore your surroundings. Hotel Makanda's own 12 acres offer the adventurer a chance to hike through the jungle on paths leading to private beach areas and inlets.

There are a wide variety of activities in the local area for those with an adventurous spirit. Choose to explore this part of Costa Rica with a horseback riding excursion, kayaking tour, or guided watercraft tour. Fishermen will delight in catching sailfish and marlin while getting a glimpse of the dolphins and giant sea turtles that call this region home. The volcanic reefs that lay beneath the waters off of nearby islands will enchant diving and snorkeling enthusiasts. If you'd like to learn more about the wildlife and vegetation in this wild and unspoiled land, nearby Manuel Antonio National Park is an excellent place to start.

Bed & Breakfasts, Villas and Inns

Here, professional guides will take you on tours of the jungle trails.

As your day draws to its close in this land of extremes, you can visit the towns of Quepos or Manuel Antonio to find a variety of restaurants, bars, and even a casino. However, gourmet food is no farther away than Makanda's own Sunspot Restaurant with lavish food and one of the best wine selections in the area. This restaurant is popular and open to the public, so reservations are recommended for dinner. The restaurant is also open for lunch.

SERVICES: A wide variety of activities in the local area are available including horseback riding, kayaking tour, guided watercraft tour, fishing, diving, snorkeling and much more.

DINING: A tropical style, continental breakfast is delivered to your room each morning. For lunch and dinner, Makanda has an onsite restaurant, the Sunspot Restaurant, offering a variety of dishes featuring Central American cuisine. The restaurant is open from 12:00pm to 10:00pm daily. Reservations are recommended for dinner.

RATES: Rates per room per night are from $175.00 to $350.00 and vary according to the season. Makanda accepts adults and children over 16 only.

If you are looking for a nature lover's paradise, then check out Windy Point Inn in Fawnskin, California. Set along side Big Bear Lake, Windy Point Inn offers only the best in outdoor recreation and wildlife enjoyment.

Guests may sit on the private boat dock and enjoy watching all the activity of the area's wildlife or the passing boats. The sunken living room offers a peaceful place to relax in front of a cozy fireplace and curl up with a good book. Fishing and hiking activities can be found along the shores of Big Bear Lake.

Windy Point Inn offers a whirlpool for two in four of their five guest rooms. The guest rooms are a homey retreat for couples wanting their privacy, and display a breathtaking view of this beautiful, mountain lake. Guests may also partake from the complimentary afternoon hors d'oeuvres. For the musically inclined, there is a grand piano located in the living room.

A country style breakfast is served daily. Enjoy French toast, eggs, and other breakfast items that are offered. Breakfast may be enjoyed either indoors or on the outside deck. Other meal options may be found nearby.

Beautifully decorated, the rooms offer wet bars, whirlpools for two (four rooms only), individual climate control, VCR, fireplace, refrigerator, private bath, and private deck. The beds range from king size to queen size and are topped off with a luxurious feather bed topper. Two rooms offer sitting areas equipped with wrap around sofas and chairs. Four rooms offer fireplaces.

For those that desire a vacation free from the hustle and bustle of the outside world, Windy Point Inn is the destination for you.

Bed & Breakfasts, Villas and Inns

SERVICES: Fishing and hiking along the shores of Big Bear Lake may be enjoyed. In-room whirlpools for two are located in four of the five guest rooms. Other options and attractions are located nearby. A grand piano is available for guests' use and enjoyment.

DINING: Country style, gourmet breakfast is served every morning with afternoon hors d'oeuvres provided. Other dining options available nearby.

RATES: Five rooms are available at a cost of $165.00 to $245.00 per night depending on days of week and room desired. Call for more information.

Adobe and Stars Bed and Breakfast Inn

Taos, New Mexico

Situated just outside the beautiful and mysterious town of Taos, New Mexico, the Adobe Stars Bed and Breakfast Inn is a striking first class establishment built in traditional adobe style. Let the soothing southwestern décor and exceptional art from local artists transport your mind and body to a state of total relaxation. Eight guest rooms of varying sizes are available, each with a private tiled bath, kiva fireplace, cozy robes, and majestic views of mountains and mesas. A generous warm breakfast is served each morning to start your day with luxury and pampering. From there, you can choose to linger in the inn, curled up by the fire with a good book, or arrange for a luxurious, in-room massage. If you'd like a brisker pace, set out to discover all that Taos and the surrounding area have to offer.

In winter, take advantage of the snowy mountains with skiing and snowmobiling. For a more romantic wintry rendezvous, consider a horse drawn sleigh ride through the countryside. Available warm weather activities include biking, hiking, and rafting. For something different, visit one of the local wineries or arrange for a ride in a hot air balloon to see the beauty of Taos from high above the earth. Explore the many art museums and studios in Taos and nearby Santa Fe, the birthplace of southwestern art. At some of the studios, you can actually meet local artists, talk with them, and view their newest work.

When it's time to stop for dinner or lunch, an array of restaurants ranging from quaint cafes to gourmet cuisine await you. Try several and note how each chef uses the flavor of chilies and other local produce to create the delicious southwestern cuisine

Bed & Breakfasts, Villas and Inns

Adobe and Stars Bed and Breakfast Inn

CONTACT:

WEBSITE:
www.taosadobe.com

EMAIL:
stars@taosadobe.com

PHONE:
800-211-7076 or 505-776-2776

ADDRESS:
Adobe and Stars
Bed and Breakfast Inn
P.O. Box 2285
Taos, New Mexico 87571

that has become popular nationwide. Be sure you're done with dinner early at least once during your stay at the inn so you can hurry back and catch the spectacular sunset views.

After dinner many find themselves enjoying a romantic evening sipping a cool drink while watching the sunset from the open-air hot tub. Twice a year Adobe and Stars offers special Yoga retreats and full massage services are also available to help you relax at any time.

The Adobe and Stars feature unique pieces from some of New Mexico's most prominent artists. Sculptures by Stiles Thissell are all around the property. Paintings by Doug Benko add flare and culture to many of the guestrooms.

Taos has 22 professional wineries. It is home to some of the oldest wineries in the U.S. attracting thousands of wine connoisseur's each year as they flock to the Annual Taos Winter Wine Festival.

SERVICES: Shuttles to the ski slopes and storage for ski equipment are available. Your host will also assist with reservations to restaurants and area attractions and can arrange for in-room massage.

DINING: A full country breakfast of homemade muffins, biscuits, hot entrée, fresh fruit, juice, and coffee is served daily in the dining room. During the summer, breakfast can be enjoyed on the outdoor patio. Afternoon snacks are also available.

RATES: Room rates are between $115.00 and $180.00 per couple and are slightly higher during the holiday season. Pets are welcome and smoking is allowed out on the patio.

Red Umbrella Inn

Minden, Ontario, Canada

Minden, Ontario is home to some of the most beautiful, riverside views. This serene setting is also home to Red Umbrella Inn. This inn is for adults only and caters to couples.

Rooms, cabins, and cottages offer accommodations that feel like home. One of the unique benefits of this quaint inn is they allow pets in some of their room and cabins. This allows you to not only have a special getaway together, but to also save the dreaded kennel fees. Pets may not be accommodated in the Victorian Rooms of the inn, however they are allowed in the Gatehouse, cabins, and cottages.

Many activities are available during the summer for guests' enjoyment, including fishing, swimming, boating, and hiking. Winter will bring skiing, sleds, ice-skating, and more. There is also a lakeside year round hot tub, three jacuzzis, a library, and game room to keep guests occupied.

Two wonderfully delicious meals are provided daily with optional dining facilities located nearby. Also nearby are museums, churches, snowmobiles, five golf courses, and horseback riding.

Couples looking for a quiet romantic retreat free from the turmoil of daily life will be pleased with this country inn. The clean air is good for the body, and the peaceful setting is food for the soul. Try Red Umbrella Inn on your next getaway. See the beauty of Ontario, Canada!

Bed & Breakfasts, Villas and Inns

Red Umbrella Inn

CONTACT:

WEBSITE:
www.redumbrellainn.com

EMAIL:
info@redumbrellainn.com

PHONE:
800-461-0361 or 705-489-2462

ADDRESS:
Red Umbrella Inn
Rural Route 2
Minden, Ontario, Canada K0M 2K0

SERVICES: Services that are provided at Red Umbrella Inn include boating, swimming, three jacuzzis, lakeside hot tub, fishing, skiing, skating, sleds, and other activities and attractions located nearby.

DINING: Two wonderfully robust meals are served daily. If optional dining facilities are desired, they can be found in the nearby town. A bar is located in the game room for those that desire an alcoholic beverage.

RATES: Rates are seasonal and range from $89.00 to $109.00 per person per night. Call for details.

Bed & Breakfasts, Villas and Inns

174

The beauty of Puget Sound is the setting for this wonderful bed and breakfast. Located on Kitsap Peninsula, Willcox House offers a lovely, relaxing and friendly atmosphere to be enjoyed on your next getaway.

All five guest rooms have a breathtaking view of Hood Canal and Olympic Mountains. Constance's room provides the warmth of a fireplace, king size bed, and single bath. Julian's room has a manly feel and is also equipped with double jacuzzi, and a separate shower. The Rose Garden room provides its guests with a queen size and twin bed and can accommodate up to three persons. It has a sitting room and single spa with shower. The Clark Gable room has a king size bed, with shower. Last, but not least, Colonel's room has a French feel to it and sports a king size bed and large shower.

Complimentary hot beverages can be found in the pub. Dining experiences are top notch. Gourmet meals are prepared using local ingredients and allow guests to experience local favorites. Other dining options may be found within one of the local towns. Also located nearby are golf courses, museums, herb farms, harbor cruises, antique shops, wineries, hiking, garden attractions, beaches, tours, farmers' markets, and local festivals and fairs.

Oysters may be found along the beaches or guests may choose to watch television in the Great Room. For those that like to have their nose in a good book, an extensive library is also provided for guests' enjoyment.

Take in the beauty and majesty of the great Northwest on your next vacation!

Bed & Breakfasts, Villas and Inns

CONTACT:

WEBSITE:
www.willcoxhouse.com

PHONE:
800-725-9477 or 360-830-4492

ADDRESS:
Willcox House
A Premier Country House Inn
2390 Tekiu Road NW
Seabeck, Washington 98380

SERVICES: Library, television, pub and poolroom are provided for guests with other entertainment options located nearby.

DINING: Hot beverages are served in the pub. Gourmet meals are offered at a cost of $21.50 to $32.50 per person. Other dining options available within the nearby towns.

RATES: Five rooms are available ranging from $129.00 to $199.00 per night with an additional $30.00 for an extra person in the Rose Garden Room. They accept children 15 years of age and older.

Key West, Florida

The southern most part of the continental United States, Key West is a tropical island paradise that is only seven square miles. Banana Bay Resort is a lushly landscaped inn that's centrally located right in the heart of Key West. It is only walking distance to the island's many festivities.

Banana Bay Resort hosts 48 guestrooms that are arranged into five two story buildings, and many of the rooms offer a private balcony. All of the rooms have air-conditioning, private baths, ceiling fans, remote-controlled color television, bathrobes, phones, refrigerators, wet bars, coffee makers, hair dryers, irons/boards and a clock radio. You have choice of two double beds or one king sized canopy bed. The suites have an extra pull out with bedding and a kitchen.

There are many activities to enjoy in Key West while staying at the resort. The Sunset Celebration is a favorite attraction of both locals and tourists when visiting. Every night, just a few minutes before the sun sets, everyone makes his or her way down to the end of Duval Street to Mallory Square. You'll find live magic, musicians, entertainers, sword swallowing, cold drinks and many vendors selling handcrafted souvenirs. And of course, you'll be able to view one of the most spectacular sunsets you'll ever see.

And for those looking for something a little more secluded, Banana Bay also offers a private island getaway for up to four adults. Pretty Joe Rock Island features a 1000 square foot luxurious cottage complete with a jacuzzi. There are two bedrooms, two baths, ceiling fans, air conditioning, television, DVD-VCR & stereo and a washer/dryer.

Bed & Breakfasts, Villas and Inns

Banana Bay Resort

CONTACT:

WEBSITE:
www.bananabay.com

EMAIL:
info@bananabay.com

PHONE:
800-226-2621 or 305-296-6925

FAX:
305-296-2004

ADDRESS:
Banana Bay Resort
2319 N. Roosevelt Boulevard
Key West, Florida 33040

SERVICES: The resort has a freshwater pool, private beach, Tiki-bar, fitness center, waterside whirlpool, volleyball court, private dock and a beachside wedding gazebo for those wishing to tie the knot. They also offer several special weekend packages for fishing, diving, weddings or exclusive romantic weekend getaways that include welcome drinks and sunset cruises for just the two of you. Snorkeling, scuba diving, private dolphin watching tours, fishing tours, coral reef tours, sailing, kayaking, powerboats, wave runners, private sunset cruises and many other services can be arranged for a small fee.

DINING: A complimentary continental breakfast buffet is served beachside daily. Numerous restaurants are within walking distance of the resort including Sloppy Joes, one of the most famous eateries in Key West. Catering service is also available for weddings or other small meetings.

RATES: Rates for the resort range from $175.00 to $250.00 per night based on double occupancy depending on the time of year you go and type of room you select. Extra adult rates are $15.00 per night, per adult. If you choose to travel by boat, they have dockage available for boats up to 24 feet for only $20.00 per night. Weekly private island rentals start at $5000.00, which can be shared by two couples if you wish.

The Watson House

Key West, Florida

Tropical ocean breezes, salt tinged air, and bright sunshine greets the guests of The Watson House in Key West, Florida. Towering palms and beautiful, sandy beaches are just a touch of the beauty experienced at this adult only bed and breakfast. Rated A+ by the American Bed and Breakfast Association, The Watson House is a wonder to behold. Restored in the 1980's, The Watson House is an ideal, cozy retreat for a relaxing vacation.

There are four suites available. The Susan Suite is decorated in white wicker furniture and offers a private bath, queen size bed, phone, cable television, coffeemaker, and refrigerator. The William Suite has a taste of the 19th century and sports a fully equipped kitchen. The Watson Suite is the Susan and William combined and is meant to accommodate up to four persons. With the incorporation of the two suites, it offers two baths and a private veranda. The Cabana is for those that wish a little more privacy in their accommodations. The Cabana has all the comforts of home, including a king size bed, kitchen, private-deck and dining area, and is located poolside. The pool is decorated with a waterfall and guests may also enjoy the large spa.

All the entertainment a guest could want may be found within Key West. Swimming, beaches, boating, fishing, clubs, dining, and shopping are all just a few short minutes away.

If the tropics, relaxation, and a homey environment are your dreams for the ideal vacation, then make reservations at The Watson House in Key West, Florida today!

Bed & Breakfasts, Villas and Inns

The Watson House

CONTACT:

WEBSITE:
www.oldeisland.com/
watsonhs.html

EMAIL:
watsonhse@oldeisland.com

PHONE:
800-621-9405 or 305-294-6712

ADDRESS:
The Watson House
525 Simonton Street
Key West, Florida 33040

SERVICES: Swimming pool with a waterfall is available for guests' enjoyment, as is the large spa. Entertainment, attractions, and shopping are all located nearby.

DINING: In-room meal preparations with optional dining facilities located within Key West.

RATES: Seasonal rates range from $125.00 to $315.00 spring/summer, $105.00 to $245.00 fall, and $140.00 to $370.00 winter. Call for details and dates.

The Honor Mansion

Healdsburg, California

In the heart of the beautiful Sonoma wine country is a unique property for those seeking a romantic escape. Built in 1883, the Honor Mansion was restored to its original elegance and offered as a bed & breakfast. There are over 100 wineries in the area that you can explore making the Honor Mansion perfect for a romantic weekend wine get-away or a wine tasting anniversary vacation.

With five elegantly appointed rooms and six suites, there are plenty of choices for your romantic escape. Each room is furnished with beautiful antiques and will take you back to a time when things were much simpler. One such room is the Magnolia Room complete with carved four-poster bed, European linens and a view of the 100-year-old magnolia tree right outside your window.

If you're seeking the utmost in privacy and luxury you'll want to choose one of their six suites. The Vineyard II suite offers guests a romantic and relaxing environment to enjoy themselves in. With features such as a see through fireplace that can be enjoyed from the bedroom or the soaking tub in the bathroom, to the private patio with whirlpool tub, you'll be completely at ease and ready for romance.

Start each day with an assortment of goodies for breakfast. Cappuccino, Cafe Latte or freshly ground coffee are all available, as well as fresh fruit and an assortment of teas. A two or three course breakfast is the norm at the Honor Mansion. Perhaps you'll want to follow breakfast with one of the many wine tours available to guests. However you choose to spend your time at the Honor Mansion, there is plenty to do and you will feel a sense of history, romance and personal attention that's hard to beat.

The Honor Mansion

CONTACT:

WEBSITE:
www.honormansion.com

EMAIL:
innkeeper@honormansion.com

PHONE:
800-554-4667 or 707-433-4277

FAX:
707-431-7173

ADDRESS:
Honor Mansion
14891 Grove Street
Healdsburg, California 95448

SERVICES: 24-hour Espresso/Cappuccino machine services, afternoon refreshments, beautiful walking gardens, lap pool and surrounding decks are available. Complimentary appetizers and wine hour for guests. Many wine tours are also available.

DINING: A two or three course breakfast is available to guests including Cappuccino, Café Latte or freshly ground coffee and fresh fruit juice. An assortment of afternoon refreshments and appetizers are also served.

RATES: Room rates range from $180.00 to $290.00 per night while suite rates range from $300.00 to $475.00 per night. Rates are based on single or double occupancy. Weekends require a two night minimum stay. This is a romantic and adult environment.

Built exclusively to serve as a bed and breakfast, the All Season's River Inn has the charm of a historic home with some surprising modern amenities. Each antique laden room has a private bath and queen bed with down comforter, and five are available with a private jacuzzi. Two-room suites and rooms with a fireplace are also available.

Perched just 80 feet above picturesque Wentachee River, the inn offers calming views of both the water and surrounding forest and wildlife, all nestled in the majesty of the Cascade Mountains. Established trails around the inn are ideal for romantic walks or an invigorating ride on one of the inn's complimentary bicycles.

Drive to the nearby village of Leavenworth for dinner or the entire day. This delightful little town will make you believe you've just stepped into a village in the Swiss Alps. Stroll the countless shops or take advantage of a wide variety of more active endeavors such as river rafting tours in summer or skiing in winter. When you're finished, be sure to stop in at one of the German-style restaurants or popular coffee houses. Whatever your tastes, Leavenworth offers a wide variety of restaurants.

Many popular festivals also take place in Leavenworth throughout the year. If you plan to visit the inn during one of these events, make your reservations early, as lodging fills up quickly. Some of the most popular festivals include the Bavarian Maifest in May, the Salmon Festival in September, and the Christmas Lighting Festival in December. Each festival offers a variety of daily activities.

Bed & Breakfasts, Villas and Inns

All Season's River Inn

CONTACT:

WEBSITE:
www.allseasonsriverinn.com

EMAIL:
allriver@rightathome.com

PHONE:
800-254-0555

ADDRESS:
Leavenworth, Washington

No matter how you choose to fill your days, at the close of each one, the beautiful All Season's River Inn will be ready to welcome you back to a warm and comfortable bed with the soothing sounds of the river just below.

SERVICES: Available services at the inn include specialized gift baskets, birthday cakes, flowers, and in-room massages. Call ahead to inquire about availability of services.

DINING: The morning meal is an important part of your overall experience at All Season's River Inn. The inn is known for fabulous gourmet breakfasts that go far beyond eggs and bacon. Breakfast is served daily in the dining room.

RATES: Room rates vary according to size and accommodations, but are generally $135.00 to $185.00 per night. Minimum stay requirements are two nights for non-holiday weekends and festivals and three nights for all holiday weekends. Multi-night discounts are available at various times throughout the year. All rooms are single or double occupancy only. Pets and children under 16 are not permitted.

Perched high atop the Southern California coast is a very private and luxurious romantic bed and breakfast. Offering a clothing optional sundeck, this is a place you can unwind both your body and mind. Average temperatures range from the 70's to the upper 80's in the summer and fall, making this an extremely comfortable environment to shed your worries and clothes. The owners' stress that clothing optional is an "option" and is not something you have to be confronted with if you desire not to. The clothing optional areas are designated. Your comfort level is of extreme importance to them and they want everyone to experience a romantic and relaxing vacation.

The Sea Mountain Ranch is a very unique property indeed, open to single women or couples, and also groups of women for special spa days. At 2700 feet above the Pacific Ocean in the mountains of Malibu, it offers guests full ocean views and wonderful landscapes all while being completely secluded in a romantic environment.

Imagine spending the day nude sunbathing with your partner as you gaze out across the expansive view from the private deck. Or perhaps you would enjoy a relaxing dip in the designer pool or warm jacuzzi. At night you may decide to relax in the ocean view whirlpool while gazing at the stars. The accommodations are something you don't often see with a property of this size. Three suites and a private lodge offer sweeping ocean views, fireplaces and the utmost in privacy. There are so many amenities for this property that we encourage you to investigate further. This is an adult only romantic experience that is worth every penny.

Bed & Breakfasts, Villas and Inns

Sea Mountain Ranch

CONTACT:

WEBSITE:
www.seamountainranch.com

EMAIL:
info@seamountainranch.com

PHONE:
877-928-2827 or 818-886-0326

ADDRESS:
Sea Mountain Ranch
9510 Vassar Ave
Chatsworth, California 91311

SERVICES: Guests can enjoy spa treatments including day and group spas. Steam shower, aromatherapy, European style tanning, natural wood sauna, whirlpool, fitness center and clothing optional tanning decks are just some of the many choices offered.

DINING: Award winning cuisine is provided with an extensive menu. All meals are brought directly to Sea Mountain Ranch through an exclusive arrangement with the number one rated deli in the nation.

RATES: There are four guest accommodations. The rate for single occupancy is between $199.00 and $375.00 and the rate for double occupancy is between $275.00 and $499.00. The rate for each additional person is $75.00. Special rates are often available. No children and no pets. All rates are per night.

Puerto Moralos, Mexico

This destination conjures up images of Jimmy Buffet's "Margaritaville". If you've been to the more tourist heavy areas of Mexico and wondered if Jimmy's dream town ever existed, look no further. Puerto Moralos is a laid back, traditional town with the sandy beaches you long for, and Rancho Libertad blends seamlessly into the backdrop. With American owners running the facility, you can enjoy the authenticity of this lazy little town with the comfort and ease of English speaking hosts.

The facility is a grouping of six two-room palapa style cabanas located right on the sand with a large, shared, beach side palapa lounge complete with kitchen. All rooms have hammock style beds suspended from ropes, ceiling fans, and spacious bathrooms. The upstairs rooms have queen beds and cost a little more than the downstairs rooms offering double beds. Some rooms are also available with air conditioning.

After indulging in the large buffet breakfast, join other guests for a relaxing day in the lounge palapa playing guitar, or games, or just chatting, or set out for the beach. Many waterfront activities are available including snorkeling excursions and diving tours. Puerto Morales is also within easy access of many of the fabulous Mayan ruins along the coast and just a short ride from Chitzen Itza, widely considered the grandest of all the Mayan ruins. For lunch, walk into town to sample one of the authentic Mexican restaurants. In the evening, consider a drive just minutes up the highway to popular Cancun. Here, you can enjoy shopping, dance clubs, and a wide variety of restaurants. Nighttime drumming exhibitions on the beach at Puerto Morales occur most months during the full moon. Buy your own at the gift shop and join in!

Bed & Breakfasts, Villas and Inns

SERVICES: Complimentary bikes and snorkeling equipment are available. Massage and homeopathy are available at an additional charge. There is a gift shop onsite featuring handmade drums.

DINING: A complimentary breakfast buffet consisting of sweet bread, fresh fruit, cereal, granola, yogurt, coffee, tea, and juice is served each morning.

RATES: Rates are from $59.00 to $79.00 in winter, and $39.00 to $59.00 in summer. Rates are per night for single occupancy. Double occupancy is available for $10.00 more per night. Rancho Libertad is for adults only except in June, when families are accepted.

Oceanwood Country Inn

Mayne Island, British Columbia, Canada

Nestled in a relaxing wooded setting along the shoreline, lies the beautiful Oceanwood Country Inn. This inn is located in one of the most magnificent areas in British Columbia and offers its guests a relaxing array of benefits.

Guests are treated to rooms equipped with amenities such as whirlpool, jacuzzi, or soaking tubs. Fireplaces create a warm and cozy feel, perfect for those romantic evenings in front of the fire. Private decks or balconies are an added bonus.

Take a stroll through the garden, thick with the scent of the many blooms bursting in their colorful display. If a little more activity is desired, bicycle riding, tennis and parlor games are available. This inn caters to adults who wish to sit back, relax and enjoy each other without a lot of physical activities to interfere. There is also an extensive library on the premises for guests' enjoyment.

Full breakfasts are included in your stay and are offered daily. Elegant, but simple, evening meals include four courses and offer only the freshest local ingredients. Steamed Halibut, Stuffed Crab, and Rack of Lamb are only samples of the delicious meals that await guests.

If you are looking to get away from all the chaos of daily life and enjoy elegant simplicity, then book your next vacation or getaway at Oceanwood Country Inn. Experience the beauty, peace, and relaxation of British Columbia, Canada.

Bed & Breakfasts, Villas and Inns

Oceanwood Country Inn

CONTACT:

WEBSITE:
www.oceanwood.com

EMAIL:
oceanwood@gulfislands.com

PHONE:
250-539-5074

FAX:
250-539-3002

ADDRESS:
Oceanwood Country Inn
630 Dinner Bay Road
Mayne Island, British Columbia,
Canada V0N2J0

SERVICES: Activities include bicycling, tennis, parlor games and garden walks. Library available for those who desire a good book to read. Whirlpools, jacuzzis, or soaking tubs are available in most rooms.

DINING: Full breakfast is offered daily and included with your stay. Simple, but elegant, four course dinners are offered at additional cost featuring local favorites.

RATES: Their 12 rooms offer guests a choice of amenities. Rates are seasonal and range from $119.00 to $329.00 per night. Call, visit their website, or email them for full details.

Mountain Memories Inn

Hiawassee, Georgia

High in the wooded mountains of northeastern Georgia sits the Mountain Memories Inn, an idyllic romantic retreat with fantastic views of nearby Lake Chatuge and the surrounding mountains. The inn offers six generous and thoughtfully decorated rooms designed to give flight to romantic fancy. Try one of the honeymoon suites complete with a bedside hot tub and king size bed, or choose a room with a cozy queen size bed. All rooms come with private bath, a robe, and candles to set the mood. Rooms with a private entrance are also available.

Each morning, a full breakfast buffet is provided in the dining room. Chat with other guests as you sit at candlelit tables finished with real china and silver and enjoy the spectacular view out the large picture window. Come back to the dining room late in the evening for a stylish dessert buffet also served by candlelight. Look out the window again and note how the light and shadows have changed to provide a completely different mountain scene.

The low-slung mountains of northern Georgia are an outdoor enthusiast's delight. Set out on one of the numerous hiking trails for a daylong adventure or opt for nearby horseback riding or golf. Journey to Lake Chatuge to rent a boat at one of the local marinas and try your luck at catching some of the bass, bream, or catfish that draw visitors to the lake each year. If shopping is your pleasure, be sure to visit the neighboring town of Helen, an old world style Bavarian village with plenty of shopping and dining to fill your days.

Mountain Memories Inn

CONTACT:

WEBSITE:
www.mountain-memories-inn.com

EMAIL:
mtnmem@brmemc.net

PHONE:
800-335-8439 or 706-896-8439

ADDRESS:
Mountain Memories Inn
385 Chancey Drive
Hiawassee, Georgia 30546

SERVICES: The inn provides a picnic basket for two by request. The heart shaped basket contains china, napkins, a tablecloth, and candle, in addition to a full fried chicken dinner and dessert. The fee for this service is $45.00.

DINING: A generous, candlelight breakfast buffet is served daily in the dining room. A dessert buffet is provided nightly in the dining room. Dinners are sometimes served on holiday nights, but reservations for these meals must be made in advance.

RATES: Rooms are $125.00 per night weekdays and $135.00 per night weekends. Mountain Memories Inn is for adults only and no pets other than service dogs will be permitted. Smoking is allowed in the outdoor areas only.

The Cottage on the Knoll

Warrensburg, Missouri

This cottage provides a private and very romantic retreat for couples in a quaint, farm setting. Don't let the rustic setting fool you. This cottage is luxurious in its amenities. Inside, you and your sweetheart will enjoy a romantic, king size, four-poster bed, a hot tub for two placed in front of a tiled fireplace, a private bathroom, a 25" TV, viewable from both the tub and the bed, and your own small kitchen. The bathroom is fully stocked with extras including hand cream, razors, tooth brushing supplies and more. Perfumed candles, bubble bath, and bath salts are available for a romantic rendezvous in the hot tub. Put one of the available romantic CD's into the stereo unit, or choose a romantic video and let your mind go wild inside the seclusion of the sturdy, cedar walls.

If you get hungry, take a peak in your refrigerator. You'll find sodas, bottled water, and a variety of snacks such as nut breads, cookies, cheese ball with crackers, fresh fruit, popcorn, or homemade salsa and tortilla chips. On the kitchen counter, there are two coffeepots, just in case you each like a different type of coffee. In the morning, you'll be served a large, country-style breakfast with offerings such as breakfast casserole, Belgian waffles, homemade biscuits, cereal, fresh fruit, homemade jellies, coffee, and tea. Lunch and dinner are on your own and you can drive into town for one of the small, local restaurants, or take the hour-long drive to Kansas City to find world-class restaurants and an abundance of nightlife.

The cottage shares the grounds with a bed and breakfast farmhouse, but it is nonetheless very secluded and a good choice for couples wanting to indulge in romantic whims without worrying about privacy issues.

Bed & Breakfasts, Villas and Inns

CONTACT:

WEBSITE:
www.cedarcroft.com/cottage

EMAIL:
info@cedarcroft.com

PHONE:
800-368-4944 or 660-747-5728

ADDRESS:
The Cottage on the Knoll
431 SE County Road Y
Warrensburg, Missouri 64093

SERVICES: The cottage provides a journal and a single-use camera to record your stay in words and pictures.

DINING: Breakfast is provided daily for the guests, as are a variety of snacks and beverages.

RATES: Standard rates are $200.00 per night, $225.00 on weekends and holidays. Additional nights are $175.00 per night. Rates are for two adults only and there are no pets or children allowed. Smoking is allowed on the front porch area only and the owners request that you not smoke in the grassy areas.

Abbey-Inn Bed & Breakfast

Brown County, Indiana

Snuggled in one of the most beautiful areas in the mid-west stands Abbey-Inn Bed & Breakfast. Surrounded by the majesty of Brown County, Indiana, this adult only inn offers all the comforts of home with the freedom from children and phones.

Their famous hot tub suites are built for a romantic retreat for any couple. The rooms at this Smokey Mountain style inn include coffeemaker, television, complimentary snacks and drinks, movies, VCR, and refrigerator. The five private hot tub suites include a luxurious hot tub for two and queen size bed. Seven rooms are simply hot tub rooms and offer what their names imply, hot tubs for two with one or two queen size beds. There are also two non-hot tub rooms available that include a full bed. All suites also offer private entrances.

Local attractions can be found in nearby Nashville, Indiana. Stroll through the famous area shopping for crafts, antiques, and gifts. Stop and enjoy an intimate dinner at any of the local dining facilities offering a variety of foods, or check out the Little Nashville Opry for the latest in entertainment and shows.

Brown County, Indiana draws thousands, possibly millions of visitors each year and is known especially for its fall foliage displays. Also known as the Little Smokies, its hillsides reflect an era of time gone by, while allowing for facilities that provide modern comforts.

If you are looking for a completely relaxing and laid back atmosphere to get away from the rigors of everyday life, then be sure to book your next stay at Abbey-Inn Bed & Breakfast in beautiful and historical Brown County, Indiana.

Bed & Breakfasts, Villas and Inns

Abbey-Inn Bed & Breakfast

CONTACT:

WEBSITE:
www.abbey-inn.com

EMAIL:
info@abbey-inn.com

PHONE:
800-669-9732 or 812-988-2397

ADDRESS:
911 Sams Hill Road
Nashville, Indiana 47448

SERVICES: While services at the inn are limited, the area provides a wealth of activities that include shopping, antiques, and hiking. All of which may be found in nearby Nashville, Indiana. No phones or children are allowed for a peaceful and relaxing retreat.

DINING: A variety of dining facilities may be found locally in Nashville, Indiana and offer a large choice of styles and flavors.

RATES: 14 Suites with private entrances are available at a cost of $80.00 to $230.00 per night.

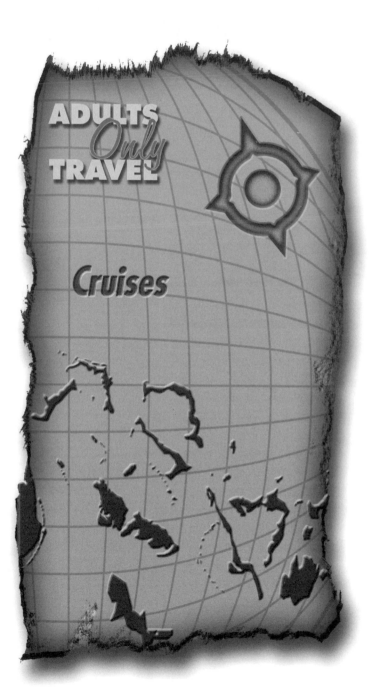

ADULTS
Only
TRAVEL

Cruises

Endless Summer II

British Virgin Islands

The *Endless Summer II* is a luxury sailing vessel offering nude cruises for up to eight people in the beautiful British Virgin

Islands. The yacht offers four staterooms, each with a private bath and shower compartment, personal closet and drawer space, and individual air conditioners for your comfort. Common areas include a fully fitted galley, and a large sitting area with bar and music center. Topside offers a spacious deck, a shaded cockpit sitting area, and swim platform complete with shower. For dining, *Endless Summer II* has its own chef serving gourmet meals and vintage wines.

The itinerary is flexible aboard the *Endless Summer II*. Guests have their say in where they want to go and where to stay the longest, etc. The cruise enjoys the calm waters and secluded anchorages of the British Virgin Islands. Available activities include snorkeling, wind surfing, water skiing, wakeboarding, kayaking, scuba diving, and hiking ashore.

Endless Summer II

CONTACT:

WEBSITE:
www.sailnude.com

EMAIL:
info@sailnude.com

PHONE:
800-742-7918 or 284-494-0384

FAX:
284-494-4731

ADDRESS:
Endless Summer II
P.O. Box 8309
Cruz Bay, Virgin Islands 00831

All inclusive rates for a seven-day cruise are $3600.00 for a double stateroom, $2700.00 for a single stateroom, and $13,500.00 for the entire yacht. Prices may be higher around holidays. Renting the whole yacht assumes no more than eight guests.

Matazz Charter

Greece and Turkey

The *Matazz* is a privately owned, 50-foot charter boat elegantly appointed, and offering week long trips with your choice of destinations in either Greece or Turkey. Your hosts, Mike and Rosie, are a husband and wife team and the boat accommodates only four guests, so you're guaranteed a very intimate setting for this Mediterranean adventure. This allows groups great freedom in setting the itinerary for each day. Meals are made on board and can be prepared to your specifications. If you have special dietary needs or a special request, it's best to give your hosts advance notice, as some foods are hard to come by in the immediate area.

Clothing optional cruises are available, but not necessarily standard, so if you're a naturist, be sure to ask if the cruise you're booking is clothing optional. Rates for a vacation aboard the *Matazz* are $5000.00 per week year round. Rates include tea and coffee, laundry, linen, welcome aboard cocktails, and transfer from hotels within 20 miles of the ship. You'll also receive full access to water sports equipment including a ski boat. Soft drinks, alcoholic beverages, and dinner are all extra.

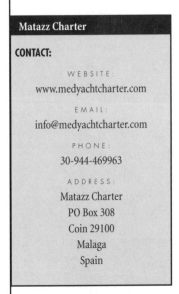

Matazz Charter

CONTACT:

WEBSITE:
www.medyachtcharter.com

EMAIL:
info@medyachtcharter.com

PHONE:
30-944-469963

ADDRESS:
Matazz Charter
PO Box 308
Coin 29100
Malaga
Spain

Dutch Love

Miami, Florida

The *Dutch Love* is a 47-foot vessel with two staterooms, and is best suited for no more than four people. The boat can be rented for charters mainly in the Florida Keys and the Bahamas. Occasionally, the crew plans special expeditions to other locations, such as Belize. The experience is very relaxed and intimate—much like being out on the water with friends. The boat is privately owned and captained by Holland native, Harman Harkema, who loves nothing more than to share his appreciation of the sea with others.

Rates for the cruise start at about $450.00 per day for the boat, crew and fuel, and the cost can be shared among up to four people. Multi-day cruises are sometimes available at a discount. Food and drink are not included. The itinerary aboard Dutch Love is flexible, but some activities you may enjoy include snorkeling, diving, kayaking, and trips to private beaches where you can be nude if you wish.

Dutch Love can also be chartered for private fishing parties up and down the coast of Florida. But most enjoy fishing off the Florida Key reefs where king Mackerel, Tuna, Grouper and Dolphin are often the catch. The on-deck barbecue makes it real easy to enjoy the fresh catch for dinner.

Dutch Love

CONTACT:

WEBSITE:
www.dutchlove.com

EMAIL:
captharman@aol.com

PHONE:
305-989-7181

ADDRESS:
Dutch Love
444 Brickell Avenue
Plaza 51-273
Miami, Florida 33131

Cruises

Caribbean Nude Sailing

St. Thomas, U.S. Virgin Islands

One of the best ways to explore the beautiful Virgin Islands is by a small charter, and even better when that charter allows you the freedom to be nude.

The charter yacht *Billy Jean* can accommodate up to five in two guest cabins, but is also well suited for a romantic trip for two. Its captain has logged over 20,000 sailed miles, bringing over 15 years of sailing experience that allows him to design your dream trip. Imagine being able to enjoy secluded spots and live some of your fantasies.

Guests may swim the beautiful turquoise waters of the U.S. Virgin Islands, walk along secluded beaches and enjoy sightseeing in exotic ports in this wonderful tropical location.

Enjoy the freedom, personal attention and complete relaxation that will come to you aboard the *Billy Jean* and your own clothing optional exploration of the U.S. Virgin Islands. Rates start at $3950.00 for two guests to $5450.00 for five guests.

Caribbean Nude Sailing

CONTACT:

WEBSITE:
www.caribbeannudesailing.com

EMAIL:
sailingnude@aol.com

PHONE:
340-690-4315

ADDRESS:
Billy Jean Charter
5100 Long Bay Road
St.Thomas 00802 USVI

Bare Necessities Cruises

Austin, Texas

Bare Necessities offers several nude cruises each year for those who enjoy a clothes free lifestyle. Take a trip from Barbados to St. Martin aboard the *Royal Clipper*, where the exact course you take will be determined daily by the wind. For a different look at the world, sail aboard the *Royal Clipper* from exotic Cannes, France to Italy and back. At either destination, with just 228 passengers aboard, you'll enjoy a luxurious sailing experience in an intimate setting where you can get to know a few people.

Bare Necessities also offers chartered nude cruises aboard the big ships from major cruise lines like Carnival. These cruises offer all the amenities available aboard the big ships, such as on

board activities and entertainment. Rates for cruises from Bare Necessities vary, but are typically somewhere between $1200.00 and $4000.00 per person, per week depending on accommodations and locations. Call or email Bare Necessities for information on a specific cruise, or to find out the departure date of their next cruise.

Bare Necessities is a great place to start if you've never had an experience with nude cruises before. They offer a very relaxed atmosphere for the novice. About 30% of their customers are first timers. They also work with some of the nicest clothing-optional adult destinations in the United States and Caribbean if you want to add a mini land retreat into your cruise itinerary.

Nubian Nile Cruises, Inc

San Francisco, California

Have you ever longed for an exotic trip down the historical Nile River? Have you always wanted to see the famous lands of Egypt, Israel, Lebanon, or Morocco? Then for your next vacation try Nubian Nile Cruises, Inc. They offer destinations such as these and more.

Step into a different lifestyle and atmosphere. Smell the scents of exotic spices and herbs that flavor the foods of these lands. Experience first hand, the differences in the lifestyles and customs that have been a part of these lands for centuries.

Nubian Nile Cruises, Inc. has several types of cruises to choose from that include one destination or packages that include several destinations. Each offers luxurious accommodations and a relaxing voyage. With this type of service, you are assured a package to suit your needs, dreams, and desires.

Nubian Nile also offers several diving cruise packages, safaris packages, romantic honeymoon packages and private yacht charters if you wanted something a little more exclusive. Full flight arrangements as well as transportation to and from the ship can be arranged for an extra fee.

Make yourself or your partner King or Queen of the Nile by booking your next vacation with Nubian Nile Cruises, Inc.

Nubian Nile Cruises, Inc

CONTACT:

WEBSITE:
www.nubiannilecruises.com

EMAIL:
info@nubiannilecruises.com

PHONE:
888-GO-NUBIA (466-8242)
or 415-440-1124

ADDRESS:
Nubian Nile Cruises, Inc.
1255 Post Street, Suite 506
San Francisco, California 94109

Cruises

No Pockets Yacht Charters

Tequesta, Florida

No Pockets Yacht Charters offer a wonderful excursion for those wishing to enjoy a totally free vacation experience. These clothing optional cruises are as laid back or as energetic as you desire.

Stroll leisurely along secluded beaches, laze back and sip champagne, or lie around and soak up the luxurious rays of the warm, tropical sun. If you want more excitement, jump aboard a jet ski, dive below the crystal clear waters, or go windsurfing.

After your day of activity, or inactivity, enjoy a wonderful meal and lively conversation with shipmates.

From the 38-foot *Lady Jane* to the luxurious 140-foot *Starship*, accommodations are of the best quality and will thrill guests. Large staterooms offer comfortable beds and the lull of the sea to rock you to a restful sleep.

Cruises are designed to fit the guest's needs and desires and allow for intermingling with others that participate in a naturalist's lifestyle. Delicious meals are served aboard the yacht and drinks are also offered. Be sure you go with an open mind if trying a clothing optional vacation for the first time and book your trip with No Pocket Yacht Charters. Once you have, you will always want to come back.

No Pockets Yacht Charters

CONTACT:

WEBSITE:
www.nopockets.com

EMAIL:
info@nopockets.com

PHONE:
561-748-5889

FAX:
561-748-5856

ADDRESS:
No Pockets Yacht Charters
341 Fairway North
Tequesta, Florida 33469

Cruises

Singles Cruises

Marco Island, Florida

If you are looking for the perfect getaway to meet other singles, then this is something you won't want to miss! Discount Travel Club offers a variety of cruises designed specifically for singles.

Attend a welcome cocktail party, captain's cocktail party, gala dinner, and theme parties. Dance nightly to musical entertainment or attend a show just like on Broadway. Enjoy beach parties, barbecues, swim in pools, soak in jacuzzis or relax and pamper yourself at the spa facilities. These are only a few of the activities available to guests on these cruises.

Lavish meals, including an extensive buffet, are provided along with 24-hour room service. All meals are prepared and served onboard and offer a wide array of delicacies.

Cruise packages vary from three to eight-nights and offer different activities and amenities, but you are assured an exciting time and plenty of other singles to meet. Rates also vary depending upon the chosen duration of the cruise package and range from $399.00 per person to $875.00 per person.

Call and see what Discount Travel Club has to offer you on your next solo vacation. Get out and meet others just like you on one of these exciting singles cruises.

Singles Cruises

CONTACT:

WEBSITE:
www.singlescruise.com

EMAIL:
cruises@singlescruise.com

PHONE:
239-393-2300

ADDRESS:
Singles Cruises
Discount Travel Club
1083 North Collier Boulevard,
Suite 150
Marco Island, Florida 34145

Cruises

The Moorings

Clearwater, Florida

The Moorings charter service offers some of the best sailing adventures in the world. Known for being a first-class operation, when it comes to helping you design your own personal dream vacation on water, there are not many who can do better. One of the best things about The Moorings is the selection and, of course, their level of personal service.

The Moorings

CONTACT:

WEBSITE:
www.moorings.com

EMAIL:
online request form

PHONE:
888-952-8420 or 727-535-1446

ADDRESS:
The Moorings
19345 US Highway 19 N # 4
Clearwater, Florida 33764

There is the option of bareboat, crewed charters or even flotillas. If you have some experience on the water and you want to handle everything yourself, then a bareboat charter is the way to go. You'll be in complete control of your adventure. If on the other hand you enjoy handling the boat at times but would prefer to have an experienced crew on board, you'll want to go with a crewed charter. Another nice experience is the flotilla. You're in control of your own boat but there is an experienced crew on a lead yacht that is there if you need them. They will guide you through some of the world's finest waters.

The most difficult thing you'll encounter with this style of vacation is where to go. There are many wonderful choices: destinations from Tonga, to the island of Corsica with six hundred miles of coastline, to Martinique and its amazing shores and much more. Choose your style of cruise, choose your destination, and give The Moorings a call and let them plan the rest. Make sure to check out their website for current rates and destinations.

Flamboyance Yacht Charters

St. Thomas, U.S. Virgin Islands

You're ready for the perfect vacation, the one you've always dreamed about. Nude sailing, snorkeling, scuba diving and sunning in a secluded cove, all while discovering the beauty of the Caribbean. Well, it's all here for you to truly enjoy that perfect vacation aboard the Flamboyance. The pace onboard this luxury vessel is designed to be relaxing and for you to enjoy what makes "you" happy. That is one of the beauties of sailing on a small charter. You don't have to succumb to the planned schedule of a large ship. This is all about you and what fantasies you want to explore with your partner.

Accompanying up to eight guests in four cabins, this 60 foot ocean schooner is ideal for couples or a group of close friends. The yacht features a main cabin that seats up to eight guests and is equipped with TV, VCR and stereo sound system. You'll also find two ocean kayaks, floating sun mats, ski tube, boogy board, full snorkeling equipment, water skis, fishing gear, deck barbecue and a large hammock for forgetting all your worries. Enjoy fresh seafood like Mahi Mahi, seared chicken, an amazing assortment of fresh fruits and expertly prepared desserts like Bananas Flambé that will make you never want to go home. You see, a trip aboard this wonderful charter with your experienced captain and entertaining hostess is much more then a typical vacation can offer. This is all about you designing and living out a custom Caribbean fantasy. Rates average $1300.00 to $1800 per person per week depending on the number of guests.

Flamboyance Yacht Charters

CONTACT:

WEBSITE:
www.flamboyance.com

EMAIL:
jim@flamboyance.com

PHONE:
340-774-5630

ADDRESS:
Flamboyance Yacht Charters Ltd.
5100 Long Bay Road
St. Thomas, U.S. Virgin Islands 00802

Cruises

Channels Charters

New Port Richey, Florida

Channel Charters offers vacationers a better choice in vacation options. Located in the Gulf of Mexico, the three level yacht is 52-feet long and offers a roomy salon area and decks both bridge and aft. Three beautifully decorated staterooms offer air-conditioned comfort, as does the entire yacht.

The yacht may be chartered from one to seven-days and can accommodate up to four people. Cruises from four to seven-days offer trips to the Florida Keys, Sanibel Island, the Dry Tortugas, or Captiva Island. All multi-day charters include all food, beverages, and fuel. Half-day trips and overnight excursions include fuel only.

This is a beautiful yacht for any special occasion or for a spur of the moment vacation getaway. With over ten years of experience, you will be assured a wonderful vacation at any of the tropical destinations. Call Channel Charters for you next vacation or weekend getaway.

For those that don't have the whole day, they also have a smaller 26-foot Pro-Cat Low Rider that is great for special half-day or full-day charters. This is a great option for a romantic sunset cruise, a unique wedding ceremony or just a fun day of nude snorkeling.

Channels Charters

CONTACT:

WEBSITE:
www.channelscharters.com

EMAIL:
info@channelscharters.com

PHONE:
727-816-9449

ADDRESS:
Channels Charters
New Port Richey, Florida

Captain Cook Cruises

Australia and The Fiji Islands

For an exotic vacation with a pirate's flare, book with the family owned Captain Cook Cruises and take a three or four-day Fiji Safari aboard a tall ship. Sailing the aqua blue waters of the South Pacific, you'll be able to explore the incredible beauty of the Fiji islands and the reef systems that abound in this part of the world. The itinerary for this adventure includes daily excursions to various islands and traditional villages. You'll be able to fish, swim, snorkel, and explore pristine beaches. There are also opportunities to learn about Fijian culture and cuisine through participation in a traditional ceremony and feast. Each evening the boat returns to Safari Village where guests stay in small huts, called bures. All meals are included.

Costs per person for the Fiji Safari are from $450.00 AUD ($230.00 USD) for the three-day cruise and $540.00 AUD ($277.00 USD) for the four-day cruise. Private charters are also available.

Captain Cook Cruises

CONTACT:

WEBSITE:
www.captcookcrus.com.au

EMAIL:
cruise@captcookcrus.com.au

PHONE:
61-2-9206-1122

Cruises

211

Windjammer Cruises

Miami, Florida

Windjammer is a small cruise line, but it also is one of the most popular cruise lines offering the small ship experience. Featuring just six vessels, five small with sails, one larger without sails, that sail to over 50 ports from the Bahamas to South America, Windjammer Cruises focus on sun, fun, and excellent service. You can choose to simply relax on board, or ask to help the crew on deck. When in port, you'll have a variety of shore excursions and water activities to choose from that vary from location to location. In addition, all meals are included in your cruise, including hors d'oeuvres and alcoholic beverages.

Windjammer Cruises

CONTACT:

WEBSITE:
www.windjammer.com

EMAIL:
info@windjammer.com

PHONE:
800-327-2601

ADDRESS:
Windjammer Cruises
P.O. Box 190120
Miami Beach, Florida 33119-0120

Singles will enjoy the special singles' cruises that Windjammer organizes each year. The staff works hard to ensure an even mix of men and women on an adventure specially designed for singles. Several of these cruises take place each year, call to find out when the next one departs!

Rates for a Windjammer cruise will vary according to ship, accommodations, destinations, and length, but a typical six-day cruise aboard one of their sailing ships is usually somewhere between $700.00 and $1200.00 per person.

Nude Yacht Charter

Mediterranean Cruises

Imagine you and your partner cruising along the beautiful waters of the Mediterranean carefree and completely au naturel. This type of getaway is exactly what Nude Yacht Charter has to offer.

Their cruises offer the best of service, accommodations, and exotic locations that cater to the naturalist. Destinations include France, Turkey, and Greece. Many of the port locations allow and encourage nudist activities.

Cruise France aboard the *Scintilla*, a 45-foot cutter that is equipped with six to eight berths. The *Cockatoo* sails the waters to the shores of Turkey. This 53-foot plus ketch, is perfect for up to seven people. Or, maybe you would prefer the luxurious schooner, *Anatolie*. The 68-foot vessel offers exotic trips to Greece and accommodates up to 12 adults.

Nude Yacht Charter

CONTACT:

WEBSITE:
www.nudeyachtcharter.com

EMAIL:
sales@nudeyachtcharter.com

PHONE:
860-442-2201

FAX:
01494-488805

ADDRESS:
Nude Yacht Charter
P.O. Box 539
Waterford, Connecticut 06385

Activities vary depending upon your destination, however most include snorkeling, beach adventures, exploration, fishing, and sunbathing. Breakfast is included in your trip, as is insurance. Other meals, fuel, and marina charges are additional costs, but the trip is worth it.

Get a taste of a different land and experience it only the way a naturalist can. Book your next nude cruise with Nude Yacht Charter and experience the wonders of the Mediterranean!

Jolly Mon Sailing

La Quinta, California

Jolly Mon Sailing is an excellent resource for finding a tailor made sailing or cruise vacation. They offer everything from trips aboard large, luxury cruise lines, to small charter trips on crewed yachts, yachts you sail yourself, and everything in between. Whatever your needs or wishes for style, price, and destination, the staff at Jolly Mon can help you find the right vacation on the water. The common bond shared by all the vacations offered is the high quality of service. You can rest assured knowing that Jolly Mon carefully examines all vessels and crews before adding them to their repertoire.

Destinations include locations such as the Caribbean, the South Pacific, the Mediterranean, Australia, and Europe. Many activities such as diving, snorkeling, and other water sports are available on many of the trips, and many of the larger cruises offer amenities such as on board casinos and entertainment. Prices and accommodations for a Jolly Mon Sailing vacation vary widely depending on the boat, location, length of trip, and other factors. Call or email Jolly Mon Sailing to inquire about rates for the trip of your choice.

Jolly Mon Sailing

CONTACT:

WEBSITE:
www.jollymonsailing.com

EMAIL:
jmsailing@aol.com

PHONE:
800-565-5984

FAX:
775-703-8397

ADDRESS:
Jolly Mon Sailing
47-815 Via Nice
La Quinta, California 92253

Cruise Nude Yacht Charters

Tequesta, Florida

Cruise Nude Yacht Charters offers, for those that enjoy the freedom of nudity, a unique ability to enjoy a completely nude cruise vacation aboard their chartered yachts. They offer a number of yachts designed to cater to adult vacations and can take you anywhere in the world. These charters are perfect for very open-minded adults. Rest assured the captain and his staff are completely discreet!

Guests will have everything aboard included in their vacation package. Activities include a relaxing hot tub, fishing, scuba diving, windsurfing, jet skiing, and snorkeling. If you'd like, the captain will find a romantic, secluded beach for a leisurely nude stroll. Meals are included and prepared aboard the yacht by the professional chef.

Your captain is an experienced seaman that will set out to only the finest locations. Chartered cruise packages are designed to fit the individuals' or couples' lifestyles and needs.

If you would like to design a memorable, adult vacation to suit your lifestyle, desires, and budget, be sure to call Cruise Nude Yacht Charters.

Cruise Nude Yacht Charters

CONTACT:

WEBSITE:
www.cruisenude.com

EMAIL:
info@cruisenude.com

PHONE:
561-748-5889

FAX:
561-748-5856

ADDRESS:
Cruise Nude Yacht Charters
341 Fairway North
Tequesta, Florida 33469

Invictus-Bahamas Charters

Bahamas

Why dream of a tranquil and tropical setting aboard your own yacht when you can sit back and enjoy exactly that without the expenses of owning your own boat. Join Captain Tom Wickenhauser on his next Bahamas excursion.

This catamaran is 60-feet long and can accommodate up to six guests and two crewmembers. The staterooms are beautifully decorated and are equipped with dual adjusting air mattresses and vanity with sink. The four baths offer separate shower stalls with seats. The catamaran is air-conditioned throughout and has satellite television, cassette player, CD player, cordless phone with answering machine, fax, and depth/fish finders.

Cruise to locations that other styles of yachts cannot go. Private, pristine beaches await you. Laze the day away in the hammock that is conveniently strung below the bow trampoline. Fish for marlin, snapper, and barracuda, or enjoy ocean kayaking.

Make a change from the norm and charter this wonderful catamaran and allow Captain Tom and his yellow lab, first mate "Hobie", to take you away on your own personally designed vacation getaway.

ruising For Love offers cruises for singles to destinations in the Bahamas and Caribbean. These programs are booked aboard various ships that will also have people who aren't part of the singles' group. However, singles that book through Cruising For Love will be grouped together. You'll have all the amenities afforded other passengers, plus access to special singles activities designed to help you meet the others in the group, including a welcome aboard party, cocktail parties, beach parties, and more. Singles aboard these cruises are generally from their mid 20s to 50s, and come from all walks of life and all parts of the country.

Cruising For Love

CONTACT:

WEBSITE:
www.cruisingforlove.com

EMAIL:
agrotman@bellsouth.net

PHONE:
866-451-5027 or 561-204-5481

ADDRESS:
Cruising For Love
P.O. Box 17474
Plantation, Florida 33318

They feature many holiday getaway packages such as a four-night Memorial Day Singles Cruise, a three-night 4th of July Singles Cruise, and a seven-night Halloween Singles Cruise. They also offer honeymoon cruises; maybe for that relationship that began on a single cruise!

Rates vary depending on the length of the cruise and the destinations. Prices for a typical three-day cruise start under $500.00 per person, and prices for a typical seven-day cruise start around $700.00 per person. Visit their website for a list of upcoming trips.

Enjoy nude cruises as well as land-based vacations to just about anywhere in the world on a trip arranged by Castaways Travel, in business since 1984. The company specializes in

one-stop shopping by offering nude cruises aboard large cruise vessels as well as smaller sailing ships, private chartered yachts and power cruises. Castaways Travel can also provide you with airline arrangements, rental cars, private tours and all full service travel requirements. In addition, Castaways Travel offers numerous independent and escorted land-based nude vacations world-

wide, including resorts in the U.S., Caribbean, Mexico, Australia and Europe. Castaways Travel represents all major nude charter operators for cruises from the U.S., Caribbean and European ports. You'll have to contact them directly to find out when the next cruise departs.

These cruises typically offer all of the accommodations of a standard cruise vacation, such as on board activities, shore excursions,

Cruises

and fabulous food, except that you're able to be nude much of the time with others who like to do the same. Rates for big ship cruises vary, but are generally between $600.00 and $2000.00 per person for a week. According to Castaways Travel, a large cross section of people of all ages, both couples and singles, enjoy these nude cruise vacations.

For a more unusual nude adventure, try a trip aboard a tall sailing ship. These smaller sailing vessels offer nude trips out of ports in both the Caribbean and Europe, where they can visit the smaller ports of call. They offer a very intimate setting where you can usually be nude

more often than you can on a big ship. Meals are comparable to those on the big ships. Rates for tall ship cruises vary, but are generally between $1200.00 and $4000.00 per person per week.

If you're interested in a small, private charter nude sailing or power boat vacation, Castaways Travel can help you choose from numerous available options. Rates for private charter cruises will vary according to the vessel, location, length of trip, and other factors, but average between $1500.00 and $2000.00 per person per week. A big plus is that you get to choose your menu items, snacks and alcoholic beverages in advance before you even depart for your nude vacation.

Cruises

Aqua Cat Cruises

Miami, Florida

The Aqua Cat is a large, luxury catamaran offering relaxing snorkeling and scuba diving cruises from Nassau, Bahamas to the Exuma Islands. The 102-foot vessel has eleven spacious cabins, elegantly appointed for comfort and luxury, as well as gracious common areas, a large sun deck, and a diving deck. Meals are served three times a day, as well as snacks and a wide assortment of beverages. Most meals feature a combination of American and Bahamian cuisine, and fresh fish and lobster is served in season.

Guests of the Aqua Cat will be introduced to the islands of the Exumas while enjoying many activities such as scuba diving, snorkeling, kayaking, or just exploring one of the many uninhabited islands. Divers will enjoy the pristine reefs and intriguing wreck sites in the area, as well as the chance to dive with sharks. Bring your own equipment or rent it. Back at Nassau, less daring guests can enjoy the shopping and nightlife. Rates for an eight-day/seven-night trip aboard the Aqua Cat are $1695.00 per person. Four and eleven day trips are also available. Approximately 90% of their cruises are for adults only and 10% of the voyages allow children 15 and over.

Aqua Cat Cruises

CONTACT:

WEBSITE:
www.aquacatcruises.com

EMAIL:
info@aquacatcruises.com

PHONE:
888-327-9600 or 305-888-3002

FAX:
305-885-3323

ADDRESS:
Aqua Cat Cruises
P.O. Box 66-1658
Miami, Florida 33266

Cruises

221

All Aboard Travel

Ft. Myers, Florida

Set sail for a romantic adventure aboard a Regal Cruise offered through All Aboard Travel. Exotic locations, sun, and fun are all yours on this regularly occurring tour, and the best part is, you can shed your clothes and enjoy the sun shining on every inch of your body. You'll enjoy the freedom of going nude during most of the charter, with the exception of when you're in port, at some meals, and in other designated areas. Best of all, you get all of the amenities of a large, well appointed cruise ship.

Many of the cruises offer theme parties each night like toga or pajama parties. Often the entire cruise has a theme such as a singles only cruise. While most of the dining areas require that you wear some clothing or wrap in a towel while dining, you have free run of the rest of the ship. Clothing is also required while docking at port if you plan to be on deck.

Destinations and locations for the clothing optional cruise vacation vary. Call to find out about the next departure date and location. Rates will depend on the specific trip and the accommodations you choose, but rates are typically from around $650.00 to $1250.00 per person for a seven-day cruise.

All Aboard Travel

CONTACT:

WEBSITE:
www.allaboardtravel.com

EMAIL:
allaboardtravelfl@earthlink.net

PHONE:
239-274-9999

ADDRESS:
All Aboard Travel
12530 World Plaza Lane, #1
Ft. Myers, Florida 33907

Sunsail USA

Annapolis, Maryland

With Sunsail the limits are as endless as your imagination. Sunsail offers an amazing 1200 yachts and catamarans in 23 countries at 39 different bases. You can choose between bareboat charters for the ultimate in freedom, luxury crewed charters as well as flotillas where you can sail in the company of up to 12 other yachts with a lead yacht complete with skipper, engineer and hostess.

For over 25 years Sunsail has offered travelers a chance to create their own first-class custom charter vacation to more destinations than probably any other such company. Whether it's island hopping in the Caribbean sunshine, cruising the aqua-blue waters of the South Pacific, or discovering all that the Mediterranean has to offer, Sunsail has a sailing experience they can tailor to suit your needs.

Sunsail USA

CONTACT:

WEBSITE:
www.sunsail.com

EMAIL:
sunsailusa@sunsail.com

PHONE:
800-327-2276 or 410 280 2553

ADDRESS:
Sunsail USA
Annapolis Landing Marina
980 Awald Drive, Suite 302
Annapolis, Maryland 21403

Cruises

Water Fantaseas

Miami, Florida

Live your fantasies in style aboard a luxury yacht from Water Fantaseas. This South Florida charter company provides very accessible boarding in Miami Beach, South Beach, Coconut Grove, Aventura, Key Biscayne, Bahia Mar, Marriott Portside Marina and other areas of South Florida. You can rest assured they can provide you with a level of service that you would expect from a luxury yacht charter company.

Water Fantaseas

CONTACT:

WEBSITE:
www.waterfantaseas.com

EMAIL:
info@waterfantaseas.com

PHONE:
305-933-4299 or 954-524-1234

ADDRESS:
Water Fantaseas
Miami, Florida

Half day, full day or term charters up to five days are available cruising the waters of Key West and the Bahamas on your choice of over 50 yachts. They really cover a broad range of available charters for different desires and income levels. Choose from an assortment of sport yachts, powerboats, catamarans, or even super luxury party yachts like their 150-passenger yacht named *Anticipation IV*.

Water Fantaseas also offers event planning to assist you in coordinating your corporate function or other parties onboard one of their charters. Anything from a light lunch to extensive feasts to accommodate 100 passengers can be prepared by their skilled chefs.

Nudity aboard their charters is also an option. Spend your dream vacation onboard a luxury yacht completely nude and experience the exhilaration of diving, swimming and playing on the open water without the confines of clothes. Water Fantaseas is there to assist you in the planning of your dream vacation aboard one of their luxury vessels. Enjoy your next adult excursion in style!

Argosy Cruises

Seattle, Washington

Argosy Cruises offers a truly romantic and unique way to tour the Seattle harbor. Whether your group is as small as ten, or as large as 800, Argosy Cruises has a ship that will offer

you a private cruise experience that's just right for your needs. In addition to a sparkling vessel and an expert crew, Argosy offers a variety of other services that can be combined to suit any budget. Full catering, boxed lunches, and beverage services are all available in a wide range of options, as well as entertainment, dancing, and more. Rates for the cruise will depend on the size of the ship, number of guests, required services, and other factors. Call to enquire about specific costs.

Argosy Cruises

CONTACT:

WEBSITE:
www.argosycruises.com

EMAIL:
sales@argosycruises.com

PHONE:
800-642-7816 or 206-623-1445

ADDRESS:
Argosy Cruises
1101 Alaskin Way
Pier 55 Suite 201
Seattle, Washington 98101

Weddings aboard an Argosy Cruise are both memorable and unique. The staff at Argosy can help you plan a cruise that will fit your style, budget, and the size of your wedding party. They'll guide you through all the details including décor, food, entertainment, and even wedding coordination. You can even choose to have the captain of the ship perform the wedding ceremony. It's best to call for wedding cruise reservations far in advance to allow proper time to plan your wedding.

Year of the Dragon

Puerto Vallarta, Mexico

The *Year of the Dragon* is a beautiful 42-foot Morgan that offers a day trip charter away from the hustle and bustle of the city.

With a maximum number of 14 guests per charter, you will enjoy a luxurious day trip along the coastline of beautiful and ancient Mexico.

Enjoy watching the wildlife. Dolphins at play, humpback whales breaching the waves, and manta rays darting about are only a few of the options.

Breakfast is light and delicious, and offers guests a chance to converse and relax while the waves break against the yacht. After a relaxing cruise, a wonderful lunch of huge sandwiches is offered. Onboard *Year of the Dragon* drinks flow freely. The open bar is always just that, open!

Take a day out of your next trip to Puerto Vallarta and spend it aboard *Year of the Dragon*. Or, if you wish, renew your vows with the captain to officiate. What a memorable occasion it will be!

Year of the Dragon

CONTACT:

WEBSITE:
www.mexonline.com/dragon.htm

PHONE:
253-862-6070 (US)
223-3109 (Puerto Vallarta)

EMAIL:
sailthedragon@hotmail.com

Cruises

227

Connoisseur Holidays Afloat

Portsmouth, England

A very unique charter experience can be found on the inland waterways of Europe. Since 1952, Connoisseur has been offering boating holidays in the heart of Europe to travelers seeking true adventure and a romantic escape. They offer 20 departure bases in six different countries including Italy, Germany, France, Belgium, Ireland and Britain. You can choose from a wide variety of boats, in fact, over 600 boats of 30 different varieties are offered.

Imagine cruising the waterways of Venice, Italy and enjoying superb food, wine, and the amazing views. You can't get much more romantic then that! Or if you prefer, enjoy your boating vacation in Britain on the Norfolk Broads with its many watermills, pubs and fantastic romantic restaurants. Whether your party is only you and your partner or much larger, Connoisseur can easily accommodate your requests.

There is no experience required for you to enjoy your vacation and charter a boat with Connoisseur nor are any licenses required, except with select boats in Germany. So if you're new to boating they will instruct you and even provide a captain's handbook to get you started. A romantic vacation aboard one of the boats from Connoisseur cruising the inland waterways of Europe, is probably one of the best ways to really experience the culture and enjoy a very different kind of vacation. Check out their website or contact them directly for current rates and information.

Connoisseur Holidays Afloat

CONTACT:

WEBSITE:
www.connoisseurafloat.com

EMAIL:
sales@connoisseurafloat.com

PHONE:
0044-0-870-774-9933

FAX:
0044-0-870-770-8010

ADDRESS:
Connoisseur Holidays Afloat
The Port House
Port Solent Portsmouth
PO6 4TH England

Cruises

Windstar Cruises

Seattle, Washington

Enjoy a luxury cruise on one of four noble sailing ships offered through Windstar Cruises. Windstar offers a variety of voyages for the discerning traveler looking for a journey that's different from standard cruise ships. These sparkling white vessels provide luxury accommodation for between 150 and 300 passengers, assuring you plenty of personal attention from the highly trained staff. Staterooms are spa-

cious and neatly decorated with comfortable furnishings, including a queen size bed. The food on board is both abundant and exquisite. In addition, you'll enjoy such amenities as pools

and massage treatments, not to mention the glorious views on deck underneath the massive sails.

Windstar Cruises are available in the Caribbean, Mediterranean, Belize, Costa Rica, Panama, New Zealand, and the Greek Isles. Other voyages may be available at various times as well. Rates will vary depending on the

Windstar Cruises

CONTACT:

WEBSITE:
www.windstarcruises.com

EMAIL:
info@windstarcruises.com

PHONE:
800-258-7245

ADDRESS:
Windstar Cruises
300 Elliot Avenue West
Seattle, Washington 98119

specific trip you choose, but the cost of a typical seven-day adventure aboard a Windstar Cruise is between $4000.00 and $6000.00 per person. Longer trips are also available.

Sail off into the sunset. Your destination could be Cuba, Key West, The Dry Tortugas, Sarasota or Captiva. Sound great? Well, this is exactly what Sail Tampa has to offer.

Charters from Tampa are available for hire from two hours to several days duration. The captain is very experienced and knowledgeable about this area and can assure you a wonderful and memorable vacation.

You will sail aboard *Dragonlord*, a 31-foot sloop that can get you into shallow water areas the bigger yachts cannot navigate. Glimpse secluded beaches and their wildlife, soak up the sun, swim in the clear waters of the Florida coastline, or simply relax and enjoy the ride.

The captain also offers instruction in sailing for those that desire to learn, at an additional cost.

Charter rates range from $75.00 per hour to $575.00 per full day. Sailing instructions are $250.00 for introductory lessons. For your next vacation, charter *Dragonlord* from Sail Tampa. It will be an adventure of a lifetime!

Sail Tampa

CONTACT:

WEBSITE:
www.sailtampa.com

EMAIL:
captbips@sailtampa.com

PHONE:
813-837-6772

ADDRESS:
Sail Tampa
6307 Selbourne Avenue
Tampa, Florida 33611

Cruises

Nude Crewz Barebuns Charter's

Caribbean

Strip away all the ties that bind, and the shirts, the pants, and the dresses. It's the only way to sail on any of these wonderful, nude Caribbean cruises.

Your crew will take you away to the exotic and tropical destinations within the Caribbean. Swim in the crystal clear waters of St. Vincent, The Grenadines, St Martin, and the British Virgin Islands. Snorkel in the buff for the tantalizing feel of the salty water against your bare flesh. Walk lazily along secluded beaches and enjoy the company of the crew that also indulges in the comfort and freedom of nudity.

Vessels are luxurious and offer comfortable sleeping quarters. The *Serendipity* is a 42-foot wonder equipped with four cabins, as is the 43-foot *Salty Cat*, and the 42-foot catamaran. Meals are prepared by the crew in the same atmosphere as the entire trip, au naturel and delicious. You will find the crew friendly and ready to provide the vacation of

Nude Crewz Barebuns Charters

CONTACT:

WEBSITE:
www.nudecrewz.net

EMAIL:
nudecrewz@shawus.com or
flombino@shawus.com

PHONE:
813-503-7595 (Florida)

your dreams. And it will be too, because the cruises are designed to suit your desires and dreams.

Go on the freedom vacation you thought only the rich could afford. Charter your next vacation aboard one of the cruise yachts offered by Nude Crewz Barebuns Charter's. You will never want to go back home!

Yacht Connections

British Virgin Islands

Yacht Connections offers a wide variety of sailing options from a number of locations world wide, including the British Isles, the Grenadines, Fiji, the South Pacific, Turkey, Greece, and others. They have at least ten yachts that provide intimate, clothing optional sailing tours for six to ten people. Enjoy the all over warmth of sunning on deck and discovering new beaches with other naturists. In addition, many of the excursions offered, focus on snorkeling and scuba diving.

Cuisine aboard a cruise from Yacht Connections is typically gourmet fare crafted by expert chefs. Each chef has his or her own style, but all are committed to excellent service. Guests are encouraged to share requests and special dietary needs will be taken into consideration whenever possible. Meal offerings will depend upon the duration of the trip.

Because Yacht Connections offers so many sailing options, here is a guideline for prices: a two-guest yacht excursion begins at $3,500.00 per week, a four-guest begins at $5000.00 per week, and an eight-to-ten guest yacht excursion begins at $9,000.00 a week. Gratuity is not included in these rates, but typically 10-20% of the charter rate is appreciated. Also, if you are traveling to the British Virgin Islands, don't forget to ask about the local government cruising tax.

Yacht Connections

CONTACT:

WEBSITE:
www.charter-yachts.com/naturist.html

EMAIL:
yachting@surfbvi.com

PHONE:
800-386-8185 or 284-494-5273

ADDRESS:
Yacht Connections, Ltd. BVI
P.O. Box 3069
Road Town, Tortola
British Virgin Islands

Cruises

Danae Cruises

Sail aboard the *Danae IV* for a very private cruising vacation based in French Polynesia. The *Danae IV* is a 50-foot vessel with two staterooms, making it perfect for one or two couples. It has a large sunning deck, comfortable galley area, and a large salon for relaxing. With the guidance of your captain, you'll plan an itinerary that is customized to your wishes. Your adventure will include destinations within Polynesia such as Tahiti and Bora Bora. Along the way, you'll discover many private coves and beaches with fabulous opportunities for sunning and snorkeling. Because you're essentially booking a private cruise and will be visiting many secluded destinations, a vacation aboard the *Danae IV* offers many opportunities for naturists to shed their clothes.

The kitchen is fully stocked and meals are prepared daily by your hosts. You're also welcome to bring aboard your own snacks or alcoholic beverages. Rates for cruises vary according to a number of factors including the length of your cruise. Call or email for more information on rates. It can take up to a week for someone to get back with you, as they may be out on a cruise and unable to return messages immediately.

Danae Cruises

CONTACT:

WEBSITE:
www.danaecruise-tahiti.com

EMAIL:
claudine.danae@mail.pf

PHONE:
689-78-38-07

FAX:
689-66-39-37

ADDRESS:
Danae Cruises
Uturaerae Marina, Raiatea
P.O. Box 251 - UTUROA - 98735
RAIATEA

Cruises

ADULTS *Only* TRAVEL

Hot Spots

The Everything To Do With Sex Show

Toronto, Canada

Usually held in October each year, The Everything to Do with Sex Show is Canada's largest upper-scale consumer related sex show. The four-day event is designed to provide

show-goers with an action packed, fun-filled, and exciting environment, whether you're a professional representing one of the large industry businesses or an enthusiastic spectator.

Exhibitors at the show represent some of the industries largest and most outrageous businesses. From fun edibles, to adult videos, to sex therapists, you'll have no trouble finding just what you need.

The show also features a wide variety of special events. You can watch a show of the industry's latest intimate fashions, get

up-close and personal with some of the worlds most distinguished adult stars, or listen to celebrity speakers. No matter what you choose, you'll be sure to have a great time at this first class event.

Spectator tickets are available before the show through TicketMaster for only $13.00 per person per day. At the door they are $15.00 each.

Mile High Club

The sky's the limit when you earn your wings by joining the mile high club. Creating your own in-flight turbulence at 5,280 feet above the earth is an experience that everyone should enjoy at least once.

Much more comfortable than squeezing into the lavatory on the late night red eye of some commercial carrier, most of these charter flights offer the privacy you desire and provide couches or queen size beds for ultimate comfort. Make the experience more festive by filming it, or rise to the occasion with your favorite friends by making it a group event.

Fee's vary depending on the carrier but usually run from about $599.00 per flight to $1000.00 per couple per hour. There are five regional private charter lines that offer this service. Check out the web site for the location nearest you.

Lawrence Sperry founded the mile high club in November of 1916 by offering flight lessons to married women. One thing led to another and the phrase, "pull back on the yoke" will never mean the same thing again.

If you're not sure what to expect or would like to see what others say about taking their relationship to new heights before you decide, the website features a section called 'Tales Of The Club'. This section highlights several stories from real couples that have joined. Most are packed with hints and ideas that you might find interesting.

AdultDex Adult Tradeshow

Las Vegas, Nevada

This major annual adult entertainment expo in November attracts both those in the adult business as well as the many fans of adult entertainment. Held in Las Vegas during the same time as the Comdex show, this event has an attendance of between 8,000 and 13,000.

For those in the adult business it provides an opportunity to show off their products, network with those in the business, and meet with fans. For fans it provides a chance to get autographs, photos, and meet with some of your favorite

AdultDex Adult Tradeshow
CONTACT:
W E B S I T E :
www.adultdex.com
E - M A I L :
Fay@adultdex.com
P H O N E :
765-651-9872
A D D R E S S :
TradeShow Productions, Inc.
4434 E. Montpelier Pike
Marion, Indiana 46953

adult entertainers. The tradeshow attracts many Internet amateur performers as well. Showroom admission is $10.00 per day, payable at the door. Visit their website for up to date information on ticket availability and show location.

Hot Spots

241

PleasureZone

Oakland, California

Every month, between 9:00pm and 2:00am, the PleasureZone parties are held at the Hotel Ibiza. An exciting playground for couples and single women where everyone is well dressed and ready to party. The women are usually found wearing their sexiest outfits. The parties are very classy and erotic with no nudity allowed.

They cater to an upscale crowd primarily in their 20s and 30s. High energy, sexually charged dancing, great music, beautiful women, and a friendly atmosphere make this a great party spot to check out.

While the PleasureZone is known for their monthly parties, they also offer special event theme parties throughout the year such as: The Red Ball, The Bikini Bash, Back to School Night, Nymphomaniacs' Halloween Ball, The Snow Ball and the Hip Hop Booty Call party.

PleasureZone

CONTACT:

WEBSITE:
www.pleasurezone69.com

EMAIL:
info@pleasurezone69.com

PHONE:
415-789-7375

ADDRESS:
Hotel Ibiza
10 Hegenberger Road
Oakland, California 94621

Buff Divers

Katy, Texas

Buff Divers is a travel club that arranges group dive trips for those interested in scuba diving in the buff. Buff Divers travel to some of the top dive destinations in the world. Typically the members are 85% couples and 15% singles, and range in all levels of diving experience. Snorkelers and non-divers are also welcome on these trips.

According to Buff Divers, they have hundreds of members across the U.S. as well as several foreign countries.

The group travels to exotic dive destinations and occupies an entire resort or dive boat where everyone can enjoy the freedom of diving nude, as well as being nude when returning to the dive destination. Membership fees are only $15.00 per year. Members of Buff Divers find the experience of diving nude to be totally exhilarating!

Buff Divers

CONTACT:

WEBSITE:
www.buffdivers.com

EMAIL:
divenaked@buffdivers.com

PHONE:
888-686-0006

ADDRESS:
Buff Divers
PMB 404
515A South Fry Road
Katy, Texas 77450

Hot Spots

Miss Nude Northaven

Brooklyn, Michigan

Southeastern Michigan's beautiful Irish Hills is home to Northaven Nudist Resort and the stage of the Miss Nude Northaven Contest. The contest is open to all women 18 years of age and older who wish to compete for over $5000.00 in cash, prizes and trophies, and the title of "Miss Nude Northaven". Contestants strut their stuff and 'bare all' for their chance to win and, of course, to entertain the appreciative crowd. Winners can enjoy vacation package prizes that include such destinations as Hedonism in Jamaica and the Caribbean Reef Club in Mexico.

Northaven Resort is open May through September and was designed for adult nudists who want to escape to a clothes-free environment while being in the company of other like-minded adults. Situated on over 44 wooded acres, the resort provides members a relaxing environment to shed their clothes and enjoy the many amenities and activities, such as nude volleyball, large pool area, live music and parties or just soaking up the sun.

You are welcome to bring your tent, travel trailer, motor home or rent one of several rooms in the main house. There is also the option of renting The Chalet, The Palace or the secluded Tree House overlooking a stream and sitting ten feet off the ground for the ultimate in privacy.

Whether you choose to enjoy the festivities at their annual Miss Nude Northaven contest or planning for a longer visit, you'll want to make your reservations early. But for sure, if you are pushed for time, plan on watching the nude contest. It is a really fun event!

Miss Nude Northaven

CONTACT:

WEBSITE:
www.northavenresort.com

EMAIL:
hosts@northavenresort.com

PHONE:
517-592-6170

ADDRESS:
Northaven Resort
11400 Waterman Road.
Brooklyn, Michigan 49230

Hot Spots

AVN Adult Entertainment Expo

Sands Expo Center, Las Vegas, Nevada

This 4-day industry event is held in January and is sponsored by Adult Video News (AVN). AVN is a leading trade publication to the adult entertainment industry. Attracting distributors, manufacturers, and fans, this show features a wide variety of adult products and entertainment. Novelty items to DVD's and everything in between are on exhibit.

You can purchase products, attend conference sessions and special events, or just socialize with some of the sexiest stars in the adult business. Whatever you choose, if it has anything to do with the business of adult entertainment you'll most likely find it here.

Hot Spots

AVN Adult Entertainment Expo

CONTACT:

WEBSITE:
www.homeentertainmentevents.com

EMAIL:
hee@advanstar.com

PHONE:
888-421-1107 or 218-723-9130

Exhibit Hall and onsite sessions are $50.00 per person for early registration and $70.00 thereafter. Day Pass "FAN" tickets may be purchased onsite or via their website.

Often referred to as Canada's lifestyles convention, this growing meeting offers much more. From exotic art to lingerie or sex toys, this gathering is an absolute must for anyone interested in the alternative lifestyle.

Held annually in August, the show attracts some of Canada's most infamous adult performers, and draws around 400 participating couples.

Thursday through Sunday rates for adult couples are $675.00 all-inclusive including room. Bring an extra couple for only $425.00 or visit one day only for $200.00. Early registrants for full weekend pass receive a $250.00 discount.

XXX-Tasy

CONTACT:

WEBSITE:
www.foxevents.com

EMAIL:
foxevents@hotmail.com

PHONE:
905-771-5156 or 877-669-5871

FAX:
905-881-5170

ADDRESS:
Foxevents Ltd.
P.O. Box 560
1057 Steeles Ave W.
Toronto, ON Canada
M2R 3X1

Hot Spots

Nudes-A-Poppin

Roselawn, Indiana

The northeast's best totally nude outdoor beauty contest, Nudes-A-Poppin, is an all out party. Attracting many exotic dancers from across the country, the contest is customarily hosted by Ron Jeremy or another adult industry legend, and offers awards for the best females in several categories.

Spectators are welcome to bring their cameras to capture the show on film and take it home as the envy of all their friends.

Events are usually held once in mid-July and once in August at the Ponderosa Sun Club. The club offers overnight camping facilities for those who want to make a weekend out of the show.

In addition to the event, the 88 acres of this intimate campground also offers nude volleyball, tennis, basketball, and a variety of other activities to keep almost anyone occupied. Get there early because this event draws a huge crowd.

Each year awards are given for Miss Nude Galaxy, Miss Nude Entertainer, Miss Nude Petite Galaxy, Miss Nude Go-Go, Miss Nude Showstopper and Miss Nude Rising Star among others. For the ladies, there are also awards for Mr. Nude Go-Go, Mr. Nude North America, Mr. Nude Entertainer and many other special awards.

For those that want to get in on the action, audience participation is encouraged for the couples nude go-go dance contest, the wet t-shirt contest, the men's underwear contest and the itsy bitsy bikini contest.

A one-day pass for single non-club members or couples runs $40.00 per day at the gate. Advance tickets are $35.00. Beauty contest registrants are admitted free provided they are over 18, have valid ID, and register before 10:00am the day of the event.

Hot Spots

Toga Joe's Temple

New Jersey

For more than 11 years Toga Joe has hosted one of the world's largest toga and lingerie parties. The toga party usually draws in about 600 couple's from around the world. Each year the couple that has traveled the farthest to enjoy the party gets free admission to next year's event.

For those who are feeling competitive, you can compete in either the hottest couple contest or the best toga/lingerie contest to win one of two all expense paid trips to Hedonism II or $5000.00 in other prizes.

Although the toga party is what made the club famous, each year they host many other comparable parties including: the Spanksgiving Day Party, a special Halloween Party, a Valentine's Day Party, and a Back to School Party each fall.

For those that like it wet, there are two Olympic size pools and a jacuzzi that can fit about 30 people at once and where fantasies sometimes run wild.

A strict appearance code is enforced for all Toga Joe's parties and admission is limited to couples or single women only and must be over 21 years old. The exact location of the event is not disclosed until you have been approved. Cost per couple is $150.00. Fees include beer, wine and a gourmet prepared dinner buffet, although most guests are partying rather than eating! Special hotel rates are available for registrants. Check their web site for complete details.

Toga Joe's Temple

CONTACT:

WEBSITE:
www.togajoe.com

EMAIL:
togajoe@togajoe.com

PHONE:
732-591-5569

ADDRESS:
Toga Joe
P.O. Box 421
Old Bridge, New Jersey 08857

Nude Volleyball

Laguna Niguel, California

Spike this! Volleyball takes on a whole new meaning when carried out in the buff. The nude volleyball club in southern California creates a whole new flavor for anyone interested in taking volleyball to the ultimate extreme.

Competitions are held from mid March to October at locations all over California and Phoenix Arizona. Held mainly in private parks and nude beaches, you'll be sure to have a ball but don't forget your sun tan lotion. Although there is no fee for most events, some parks require a $3.00 per car day pass. Check the online schedule for dates and locations.

Nude Volleyball

CONTACT:

WEBSITE:
www.nakedvolleyball.com

EMAIL:
info@nakedvolleyball.com

PHONE:
714 643-9790

ADDRESS:
28175 Via Luis
Laguna Niguel, California 92677

The Naked City

*Tour Provided by Through Our Eyes Travel
Cap d' Agde, France*

Walk on the natural side with this dream vacation to The Naked City, Cap d' Agde, France. This fully escorted tour allows guests to enjoy a seven-day vacation au naturel in the world's only nudist city, then off to either Paris or Nice on the French Riviera for three more days!

Claudine Tartanella, the French born owner of Through Our Eyes Travel, Inc. along with her husband Paul, invite you to be among 40,000 nude bodies in The Naked City.

There are activities galore in the city. More than 50 local restaurants are ready to allow visitors to enjoy various types of cuisine in a beautiful Mediterranean location. The warm and inviting sandy nude beach stretches three magnificent miles. There are nightclubs, three shopping malls, cafes, and bistros. All are totally au naturel!

Tour packages include free chaise lounge and umbrella on the beach, two free dinners, a CD containing pictures of your trip,

live entertainment, fashion shows, swimming pool, and one night limo service to Port of Agde with Casino and Amusement Park. Accommodations include an apartment or studio with a balcony 100 feet from the Mediterranean Sea.

Also available are tennis courts, bicycling, fishing, golf, sailing, scuba diving, rollerblading, and sunbathing. There is something for everyone on this escorted, adult tour. The benefits are too numerous to mention. Be sure to check out the website or call for details. Deposits are required, however they do have an "Easy Pay Plan" that will make it possible for nearly anyone to enjoy this unique getaway! They also have a unique CD of Cap d'Agde with over 1,000 JPEG's and 9 MPEG's available for $15.00.

CONTACT:

WEBSITE:
www.cap-d-agde.com

EMAIL:
travel@cap-d-agde.com

PHONE:
908-229-3953

ADDRESS:
Through Our Eyes Travel, Inc.
4452 Cypress Mill Road
(Cypress Cove)
Kissimmee, Florida 34746

Hot Spots

Crobar, the Nightclub

Chicago, Illinois

This hard rockin' palace will set your nights on fire and wear your dancing shoes out! Crobar, the Nightclub, located near the Kennedy Expressway and North Avenue, is a hot spot no fun loving adult should miss.

People from all walks of life are welcome, however the majority of the patrons at this exciting club are living alternative lifestyles.

Hard banging music will drift to your ears as you approach this establishment. As you walk through the doors, your feet and body will take over as the music completely washes over you. It will begin with a nodding head and then turn into a writhing, twitching frenzy, as you are completely lost in the atmosphere.

The people here are hard-core fun lovers that will welcome you into their surroundings and lifestyles. The entertainment is of the highest quality. Names like Curt Caris and Carl Cox grace the stage with their talents, entertaining the swarms of partygoers.

Next time you are in Chicago, or if you live there, take a night on the town and check out Crobar, the Nightclub. It will be an experience you will never forget!

Crobar, the Nightclub

CONTACT:

WEBSITE:
www.crobarnightclub.com

EMAIL:
crobar1543@earthlink.net

PHONE:
312-413-7000

ADDRESS:
Crobar, the Nightclub
1543 North Kingsbury
Chicago, Illinois 60622

Hot Spots

The Exotic Erotic Ball

San Francisco, California

With over 21 years of experience, the host of the Exotic Erotic Ball knows how to put on a quality show. Over the years, this fetish ball has been featured on E-Channel many times, and has become world renowned as one of the most exotic Halloween parties around the world.

At the worlds largest annual erotic fetish ball it would not be uncommon to see a famous movie or sports figure, or perhaps your favorite adult star. This is one hot party you don't want to miss.

Attendees can choose from general admission tickets starting at only $25.00

The Exotic Erotic Ball

CONTACT:

WEBSITE:
www.exoticeroticball.com

E-MAIL:
karin@exoticeroticball.com

PHONE:
415-567-BALL

ADDRESS:
San Francisco, California

each or choose a VIP admission package for $55.00. VIP admission includes; no waiting in line, free exotic erotic gear, preferred seating, and complete access to the backstage VIP lounge area where you can mingle with the stars.

Fantasy Fest

Key West, Florida

What could be better than a vacation in Key West, Florida, you ask? Well, how about a very special event in Key West that draws thousands to the hottest vacation spot each year?

Fantasy Fest

CONTACT:

WEBSITE:
www.fantasyfest.net

EMAIL:
kwfanfest@aol.com

PHONE:
305-296-1817

ADDRESS:
Fantasy Fest
P.O. Box 230
Key West, Florida 33041

The Fantasy Fest is an experience of a lifetime. Created around a theme each year, costumes, music, fun, and frolic fill the air. The theme for 2001 is based on astrology and the zodiac. Costumes of bright colors reflecting the signs of the zodiac and celestial bodies will prance about in the excitement of the event.

This annual ten-day and night event will start off with a royal coronation in which the king and queen of the fest will be crowned. Then, each day new events and activities will allow visitors to enjoy all this wonderful festival has to offer. Parades of Tarot card readers, palm readers, and healers will be on hand for the event. Other activities included in this festival are a masked ball, headdress ball, yacht race, talent show, celebrity look-a-like contest, toga party, street fair, and an art show unlike any other. This art show is for those that love body art! The Fanasty Fest will wrap up with a Tea by the Sea on the last evening. This is a full evening of music, dancing, and fun!

New Zealand Wedding Services, Ltd.

New Zealand

If you are a couple planning to get married, then check out New Zealand Wedding Services, Ltd. They offer wedding coordination and exciting wedding packages for couples that would like to have their wedding in beautiful New Zealand.

Imagine your wedding in a beautiful wheat field, complete with a magnificent floral display. Or, how about in the famous Glow Worm Caves, let these little creatures help illuminate your ceremony. For the golf lover, they can plan your wedding ceremony at a wonderfully luxurious golf course. And for those with a more extreme desire in tying the knot, try the Bungee wedding or a nude wedding.

Services provided by New Zealand Wedding Services, Ltd. include license, desired setting, official to perform ceremony, and two witnesses. Some other options include an organist for church affairs, flower bouquets and boutonnieres, bridal car transfer, sparkling wine, unity candle, reception planning, accommodation arrangements, and grooming.

Before you start planning your wedding, think about the beauty and atmosphere that only New Zealand can offer. Call New Zealand Wedding Services, Ltd. and let them plan an event you will never forget!

New Zealand Wedding Services, Ltd.

CONTACT:

WEBSITE:
www.nzweddingservices.co.nz

EMAIL:
info@nzweddingservices.co.nz

PHONE:
64-3-359-3993

FAX:
64-3-359-3998

ADDRESS:
New Zealand Wedding Services, Ltd.
PO Box 14037
Christchurch 8001
New Zealand

Hot Spots

Lifestyles Convention

Any open minded adult will enjoy this event, but for couples involved in the lifestyle, or swinging, a trip to the annual Lifestyles Convention is guaranteed to be a good time. You'll enjoy strolling through dozens and dozens of exhibits from adult oriented companies including sexy clothing lines, adult toys, adult resorts, and more. Special exhibitions such as erotic art and the Mr. and Ms. Lifestyle contest are also sure to be fun.

People at this event probably don't need any help getting to know each other, but just in case, the organizers have arranged several sexy party opportunities at each convention such as the favorite Very Naughtie Nightie party to ensure plenty of good occasions for mingling. For the slightly more serious set, there are also several seminars covering a wide variety of issues dealing with sexuality, sensuality, and various alternative lifestyles.

One of the unique events the show offers is the Sensual & Erotic Art Exhibition that usually starts on the second day. It features art from over 30 artists who display their erotic concepts with paintings, sculptures and other art pieces. Another favorite is the Topless Bowling Party that usually takes place on the third or fourth day.

Contact The Lifestyles Organization by phone or email, or visit their website for more information on the next convention location and schedule.

Lifestyles Convention

CONTACT:

WEBSITE:
www.lifestyles-convention.com

EMAIL:
info@PlayCouples.com

PHONE:
714-821-9953

ADDRESS:
The Lifestyles Organization
2641 W. La Palma Ave #F
Anaheim, California 92801

Exotic Dancer Fan Fair

Las Vegas, Nevada

Brought to you by the publishers of Exotic Dancer Magazine, this is a two-day event any adult entertainment fan should make time for. This is your chance to meet beautiful centerfolds, cover girls, and adult film talent, up close and personal.

Enjoy watching a huge parade of lovely ladies in the world's largest Bikini Contest and party the night away at evening festivities. You'll also have many opportunities to meet your favorite talent during the day at the tradeshow and snap your own photos to show your friends back at home. This is an annual event. Check their website for dates and times of the next show.

Exotic Dancer Fan Fair

CONTACT:

WEBSITE:
www.exotic-dancer.com

EMAIL:
edpublishing@earthlink.net

PHONE:
608-846-2698

ADDRESS:
ED Publications
2431 Estancia Blvd., Bldg. B
Clearwater, Florida 33761

Hot Spots

WeddingDreams.com

North Las Vegas, Nevada

Planning your wedding can be the hardest part of getting married. Your family argues over who sits where, what meals to serve, and where relatives will stay. Shake off the norm and let WeddingDreams.com handle your wedding arrangements in a lavish setting with a custom package to suit your wedding dreams.

WeddingDreams.com specializes in custom wedding planning and packages that will make your memorable event even more memorable. Imagine exchanging your vows soaring high above the beauty of the Las Vegas valley. The flight lasts about an hour, so there is more than enough time to say the words, toast your union and still take in the exciting view.

Maybe you would rather dress like the ladies and noblemen of Camelot. Prancing around in the dress of the era and feel like true royalty. Are you into space? Then, how about an intergalactic wedding, complete with space suits?

For those that would like a more exciting event, take your vows from the end of a bungee cord, diving off a high point, screeching down to the end of the rope, only to be yanked back in the knick of time. Another option might be soaring freely from a plane. You can actually take your vows while skydiving. Wow, what a rush!

Before you start planning your wedding, give the folks at WeddingDreams.com a call. They will come up with the ideal wedding that is just right for you.

WeddingDreams.com

CONTACT:

WEBSITE:
www.weddingdreams.com

EMAIL:
Questions@weddingdreams.com

PHONE:
888-293-3658 or 702-432-1077

ADDRESS:
WeddingDreams.Com
1631 West Craig Road #9-144
North Las Vegas, Nevada 89032-0219

Circus Night Club

Chicago, Illinois

ircus is one of Chicago's newest and trendiest nightclubs. If you're looking for a fun place with a great theme and a stylish crowd while in the Windy City, Circus should be near the top of your list of possibilities. The club is very large, but also very popular, so you'll want to arrive early to avoid waiting in line. Parking is tough, but there is a paid lot a few yards away and a valet is available if you'd rather pay a little more and avoid the walk.

Once inside, you'll see that much care—and cash—was put into making this a top-notch establishment. All the furnishings and decorations are of high quality. Rather than a child-like Ringling Bros. styled theme, the décor is more reminiscent of Europe's Cirque Du Soleil, complete with performance artists. There are five bars available from which you can order mixed drinks or bottled beer. The dance floor is large and filled with well-dressed patrons who obviously appreciate the emphasis on excellence here. The perimeter of the dance floor provides a space that's perfect for sitting and watching the action while you decide whom you're going to try to talk to next. Of course, you may just want to use body language, because the sound system is both very good and very loud.

Circus Night Club

CONTACT:

WEBSITE:
www.circuschicago.com

PHONE:
312-266-1200

ADDRESS:
Circus Night Club
901 W. Weed Street
Chicago, Illinois 60622

Hot Spots

Ecstasky Air

Beverly Hills, California

Thirty-five thousand feet and rising…Ecstasky Air is the world's first exotic airline where the scenery inside the plane is better than outside. Sexy flight attendants give a new meaning to in-flight entertainment wearing nothing more than skimpy lingerie.

A bachelor party favorite, the airline specializes in personalized trips and goes all out to make it a memorable experience. In-flight services include a full service spa featuring manicures, pedicures, foot rubs, facials and soothing massages. Other services include exotic entertainment, custom prepared gourmet meals, full service bar, champagne with strawberries and best of all, sexy flight attendants in lingerie catering to your every desire. And don't worry about transportation to and from the airport. Limousine service is included and brings you right to the plane. So forget about having to call a taxi or waiting in line at the airport. Just call Ecstasky Air.

And for those women that feel left out, Ecstasky Air also offers flights with your choice of muscle bound male attendants in tight fitting gear to wait on your every need.

The airline operates approximately 30 Lear and Gulfstream jets all offering comfortable first-class seating and will take you anywhere in the world that you want to go. Rates vary depending on destination and services provided. The average price for a full service round trip flight between New York and Los Angeles is about $4000.00.

Ecstasky Air

CONTACT:

WEBSITE:
www.ecstasky.com

EMAIL:
info@ecstasky.com

PHONE:
310-858-5700

ADDRESS:
Ecstasky Air
9440 Santa Monica Blvd. Suite 330
Beverly Hills, California 90404

Erotica L.A.

Los Angeles, California

If you want to visit one of the largest U.S. adult entertainment industry events of the year, you need to make the trip to Erotica L.A. At this convention, the word exhibitor takes on a whole new meaning! Since 1997, this show has grown to bring in over 20,000 visitors looking for a chance to meet and talk with dozens of erotic business owners and entertainers at the Los Angeles Convention Center. You'll have the chance to browse through vendor exhibits includ-

Erotica L.A.

CONTACT:

WEBSITE:
www.erotica-la.com

ing, erotic toys, clothes, videos, photography and more. If it's a sexy and fun product or service, you'll probably see it, and you'll have a chance to be the first to see the very newest products. Best of all, you'll also have the opportunity to buy many products right off the floor.

This is an annual event and is the last event to be held during "Adult Week." There is the "Adult Novelty Manufacturers Expo," the "Golf Tournament to Benefit Free Speech" and the "Night of the Stars." Check Erotica L.A.'s website for the dates and times of their next show and information about the other events during "Adult Week." Erotica L.A. usually has a special deal with at least one hotel if you need lodging during the convention. There is no pre-registration available. You must purchase your tickets at the door or at an authorized retail outlet listed on the Erotica L.A. website.

European Body Painting Festival

Austria

The Body Painting Festival in Austria is simply amazing. Many people have seen some form of body painting before, but until you attend this unique festival you most likely have never seen it taken to this level of art form. The annual four day event is usually held at the end of July or the beginning of August, and brings artists from all over the world to compete for cash and prizes as well as trade tips and share in their passion for this fantastic form of art.

This event held at beautiful Lake Millstättersee is open to the public and draws enthusiasts and artists alike. There are workshops if you wish to start learning how to body paint, entertainment and music, photo opportunities, contests, and some truly amazing body painting performances. Visit their website or contact them for more information and details on the next festival.

European Body Painting Festival

CONTACT:

WEBSITE:
www.bodypainting-festival.com

EMAIL:
alex@bodypainting-festival.com

PHONE:
04762/81210 International dialing code: 0043/4762

ADDRESS:
European Body Painting Festival
c/o Seeboden Touristik GmbH
Alex Barendregt
Hauptplatz 1
A-9871 Seeboden

Realize your nightlife dreams at the hottest nightclub in Acapulco, the Andromedas!

Featuring the wildest, hottest and best dance music around, the Andromedas is a once in a lifetime after-hours dance club.

As you step inside, you'll feel like you're joining an underwater party complete with a giant water playland with its own sexy mermaids. Follow the sounds of the pulsating dance beats and your mind and soul will energize your body to dance the night away like never before. Visitors will thrill at the special events, stage shows, live music and international partygoers. You're assured a wild and fun time!

Step out into the nightlife of Andromedas on your next visit to Acapulco, Mexico. It will be the highlight of your stay.

Andromedas

CONTACT:

WEBSITE:
www.andromedas.com.mx

EMAIL:
andromedas@andromedas.com.mx

PHONE:
01-7-4848815 or 01-7- 4848816

ADDRESS:
Andromedas
AV. Costera Miguel Aleman
Acapulco, Mexico

Hot Spots

Glamourcon

Taking place several times, in various places within the United States, Galmourcon is an event that's sure to please lovers of this art form. Celebrating glamour arts, Glamourcon has the best of the best in celebrity glamour guests. Guests have included Shannon Tweed, many of Heff's beautiful Playmates from across the years, and plenty of pinup models.

This event also attracts vendors that feature photos, videos, autographs, pin-up art, books and trading cards. Visitors of the event will be thrilled to be able to see, talk with, and photograph their favorite pin-up stars. This is a wonderful place to add to your current pinup collection, or start one.

Glamourcon events are for adults, 18 years of age and older. It takes place at various hotels across the U.S., so reservations are a must. Tickets for just the event can be purchased at the door. There is also another event, similar to Glamourcon that allows visitors to see, meet and photograph their favorite pin-up models from the past and present. This event is called Vintage and Modern Pinup Show, and is also held periodically across the country.

If you would like to see your favorite pinup, up close and personal, then reserve your room at the next of either of these events.

Glamourcon

CONTACT:

WEBSITE:
www.glamourcon.com

EMAIL:
glamourcon@aol.com

PHONE:
425-821-1760

ADDRESS:
Glamourcon
PO Box 2594
Woodinville, Washington 98072

AVN Adult Video Awards Show

Las Vegas, Nevada

S in City is the home of this now famous adult video awards show. Entertainment Weekly called it the "Oscars of Adult". Over the years this adult show has grown to become a star-studded event complete with live music, erotic entertainment, and includes every major star in the adult business, as well as many well-known Hollywood celebrities.

Every January the top performers in adult video and film are honored and the town buzzes with excitement and parties.

AVN Adult Video Awards Show

CONTACT:

WEBSITE:
www.avnawards.com

Drawing around 3000 attendees each year means, that if you're over 21 and a fan of adult entertainment, you'll want to get your ticket early. Admission is $225.00 per person or $1995.00 for a table of ten. You'll have to visit their website for current locations to purchase your tickets.

Fetish and Fantasy Halloween Ball

Las Vegas, Nevada

They don't call Las Vegas Sin City for nothing. The Fetish and Fantasy Halloween Ball is going on its eighth year as one of the most exotic Halloween parties in the world. This

extravagant all night party was named as "One of the Top Ten Events in the World" by the Travel Channel and by Maxim Magazine as one of the "100 Things to Do Before You Die".

The party is usually held a few days before Halloween and brings in over 5000 uninhibited costume bearing participants and is growing every year. Live entertainment is also provided throughout the evening. If you somehow manage to get bored looking at all the wild and erotic costumes and watching the shows, the event has numerous bars set-up to keep your party juices flowing as well as every kind of vendor that you can imagine.

Make sure you dress to impress to have your chance

to win the $1,250.00 cash prize for best costume. There is also a $750.00 prize for second place, $300.00 for third, $200.00 for fourth and, $100.00 for fifth place. And don't forget to bring your camera as you can take as many snapshots as you'd like.

There are three different categories of tickets available. General admission tickets are $50.00 per person, late night admission are $30.00 and allow you access from 1:30am to 4:00am. There are also after-hour tickets available for those who want to attend from 3:00am to 10:00am. You must wear a costume otherwise you will have to pay an additional party pooper fee of $25.00 to gain admittance. There are some dress code limitations so check the website for full details.

There are several other Fetish and Fantasy events during the year including a Valentine's Day ball, a mid-summer all-night bash and a Fetish Night party on the second Saturday of every other month.

Fetish and Fantasy Halloween Ball

CONTACT:

WEBSITE:
www.halloweenball.com

E-MAIL:
info@halloweenball.com

ADDRESS:
LVFFHB
505 E. Windmill
#1B-188
Las Vegas, Nevada 89123-1870

Hot Spots

The Sex Maniacs Ball

London, England

If you are looking for something very different to do and see, and would like to enjoy the company of other adventurous adults, then you absolutely must check out The Sex Maniacs Ball.

Started in 1986, this annual event takes place in London, England at different locations. It began "as an international get-together for people who enjoy erotic experimentation."

Organizers of the Sex Maniacs Ball plan their event to "stretch your imagination and provide a new environment for erotic fun and games." Each yearly event has a theme so attendees must dress for the occasion. The organizers of the ball even assist you in finding that special costume. They give everyone attending their event a guide called the "Book of Delights" which outline not only costume tips, but information helpful for enjoying yourself at this event.

You will be in the company of one of the wildest party groups you will ever experience, and one of the most memorable! No matter what sex, creed or color you are, or what your sexual preferences are, you will feel welcomed at this event. Singles, couples, gay, lesbian, straight and bi-sexual all attend this erotic gala event. There are rules to follow, only to allow everyone a good time. Some to mention are no street clothes, press is not allowed at the ball, nor are cameras. Also, any and all activities must be consensual!

This is one of the safest places to try any of your wildest desires and dreams. There are also erotic awards handed out for a variety of categories, including Erotic Performer of the Year.

Celebrating the beginning of Spring,
on Saturday 19th March 1994,
in amongst London's Docklands:

the
safer
PLANET
SEX
ball

featuring
the Terminatrix Experience

For a walk into a completely different realm, call and get your tickets for this year's Sex Maniacs Ball. It will be the experience of a lifetime.

SEXPO

Sydney, Australia

Not just another sex show "down under," although that is the spirit of the event, Sexpo in Australia hosts a wide array of exhibitors in almost every industry. Sexpo is "not an exhibition only about sex" but includes health, sexuality and lifestyles for adults.

While at Sexpo, you can enjoy fine wine at one of the many wine tastings, see the latest in home electronics or marine sports equipment, meet some of Australia's best hair or make-up artist, or check out the displays of adult fashions or tattoos. Participants can try out exercise equipment, book your next holiday at an exotic resort, or simply watch one of the many enticing stage shows.

The event is one of Australia's largest expositions. Thousands of attendees visit Sexpo during a four-day event held twice a year, once in July and again at the end of November. Opening day is always ladies day. Every lady who enters receives a free "toy" and all shows on opening day are also slanted toward the ladies.

A limited supply of free passes are available each year through their website. For those who are unable to secure a free pass, tickets cost $19.00 each. No one under 18 years of age is permitted into the show.

Club Deep

Miami, Florida

If you are looking for one of the most unique nightclubs in Miami, then try out Club Deep.

Only at Club Deep, can you twist, turn and spin on top of a two thousand-gallon aquarium. Known to frequent visitors as "Dancing on Water", Club Deep also offers the best and hottest dance hits in the country. The tunes are projected out by a state of the art, high quality sound system that rivals all others.

Famous for the ability to dance on water, Club Deep has hosted some very famous people. Sugar Ray Leonard, Jr., Tito Puente, Jr., Mark Curry and Ron Mercer are only a few of the famous celebrities that have crossed the threshold at Club Deep.

Club Deep is not only famous locally and nationally, being highlighted on the "Travel Channel" and the BBC has also given it international acclaim as well.

Regular and guest disc jockeys keep the tunes flowing through the quality sound system to the thrill of dancers. Special events that include fund-raisers, fashion shows, record release parties, corporate parties, and contests keep visitors entertained and involved. The owners will even take the time to visit with you and treat you like a life-long friend!

If your nightlife activities must include a throbbing, pulsating beat, then be sure to drop by and enjoy yourself at Club Deep the next time you are in Miami. It is an experience you will not soon forget!

Club Deep

CONTACT:

WEBSITE:
www.clubdeep.com

EMAIL:
staff@clubdeep.com

PHONE:
305-532-1509

ADDRESS:
Club Deep
621 Washington Avenue
Miami, Florida 33139

Hot Spots

Adult Travel Resources

This select listing contains agencies that specialize in different types of adult travel adventures. For an expanded listing, visit our website at: www.adultsonlytravel.com

We always recommend you use a knowledgeable travel agent where applicable, to book your trips. Whether you prefer one of these specialty agencies or another of your choosing, they almost always can locate better rates then you can on your own, and their wealth of knowledge can be extremely helpful.

Castaways Travel is a full service travel management company for clothing optional and adults only vacations, cruises, groups, charters, and private functions. Their parent company is American Express/Fox Travel.

Website:	www.castawaystravel.com
Phone:	281-362-8785
Reservations:	800-470-2020
Fax:	281-363-0916
Email:	info@castawaystravel.com
	CASTAWAYS TRAVEL,
	25701 IH-45 North,
	Suite #3A
	Spring, Texas 77380

Bare Necessities Tour & Travel offers first class clothing optional vacation packages for cruises and resorts.

Website:	www.bare-necessities.com
Phone:	512-499-0405 or 800-743-0405
Fax:	512-469-0179
Email:	scott@bare-necessities.com
	Bare Necessities Tour & Travel
	904 West 29th Street
	Austin, Texas 78705

Go Classy Tours handles reservations for couples and singles interested in clothing optional Caribbean resorts.

Website:	www.gonude.com
	www.caribbean-hideawys.com
Phone:	800-329-8145 or 888-825-2779
Email:	goclassy@goclassy.com

A&S Travel Center of Florida is a full service travel company that specializes in adult vacation packages including many lifestyle vacations.

Website:	www.astraveloffl.com
Phone:	866-221-3275
Email:	AnnMarie@ASTravelcenter.com

Lifestyles Tour and Travel is a full service travel company that specializes in escorted exotic tours for couples.

Website:	www.lifestyles-tours.com
Phone:	714-821-9939 or 800-359-9942
Fax:	714-821-1465
Email:	tour-info@lifestyles-tours.com
	Lifestyles Tour and Travel
	2641 West La Palma Avenue, Suite A
	Anaheim, California 92801

Charter Harder Tours is an exclusive VIP private charter bus company specializing in 21 and over adult only tours. These are alternative lifestyle tours.

Website:	www.charterharder.com
Phone:	626-575-3591
Email:	info@charterharder.com

Fantastic Voyages specializes in vacation packages to clothes-free and resorts in Jamaica, St. Martin, Bonaire and Mexico. Properties include SuperClubs, Couples, Solare Desert Sun, Sunset Beach, Club Orient and Sorobon Beach resorts.

Website:	www.nudetours.com
Phone:	817-568-8611
	Fantastic Voyages
	P.O. Box 681
	Crowley, Texas 76036

A Bare Affair offers nude resorts and resorts with clothing optional beaches for adult only Caribbean vacations.

Website:	www.bareaffair.net
Phone:	888-339-FUNN or 800-536-FUNN
Email:	Admin@ResortQuote.com
	All-Inclusive Resort Travel Inc.
	3267 North State Road 7
	Margate, Florida 33063

All The Way Travel specializes in all-inclusive Caribbean vacations and honeymoon packages at low prices.

Website:	www.allthewaytravel.com
Phone:	904-620-8446 or 800-344-3043
Email:	David@allthewaytravel.com

Peng Travel provides naturist holidays in America, Europe, and the Caribbean.

Website:	www.pengtravel.co.uk
Phone:	+44-1708-471 832
	Peng Travel Ltd
	86 Station Road
	Gidea Park, Romford
	Essex RM2 6DB, UK

Leisure Quest Travel specializes in organizing travel that caters to those seeking adult-only and luxury vacations.

Website:	www.LeisureQuestTravel.com
Phone:	727-571-2273 or 866.571.2273
Email:	info@LeisureQuestTravel.com
	Leisure Quest Travel
	10500 Ulmerton Road
	Suite 726-105
	Largo, Florida 33771

Exotic Honeymoons offers romantic honeymoon packages in Costa Rica. Their pre-designed packages include the most intimate beach resorts, jungle and volcano lodges. Let them help you design the honeymoon of your dreams.

Website:	www.exotic-honeymoons.com
Phone:	506-215-2412
Fax:	506-215-2415
Email:	info@exotic-honeymoons.com
	Exotic Honeymoons
	San José, Costa Rica

Discount Travel Club Singles Cruises is a full service agency that specializes in organizing singles cruises at unbeatable prices.

Website:	www.singlescruise.com
Phone:	239-393-2300 or 800-393-5000
Email:	cruises@singlecruise.com
	Discount Travel Club
	1083 N. Collier Boulevard, Suite #150
	Marco Island, Florida 34145

Through Our Eyes Travel specializes in escorted tours to the "Naked City" in Cap d'Agde, France. They also have unescorted trips available.

Website:	www.cap-d-agde.com
Phone:	908-229-3953 or 407-870-0827
Email:	paulcsr@prodigy.net
	Through Our Eyes Travel, Inc.
	4452 Cypress Mill Rd. (Cypress Cove)
	Kissimmee, Florida 34746-2760

Caribbean Hideaways is a full service agency that exclusively offers clothing optional and clothes free naturist vacations. They provide full travel services including land packages and air travel.

Website:	www.caribbean-hideaways.com
Phone:	800-329-8145
Fax:	727-784-4284
Email:	skinny-d@skinny-dip.com
	Caribbean Hideaways, Inc.
	2676 West Lake Road
	Palm Harbor, Florida 34684

Adults Only Travel Resources

All Aboard Travel specializes in cruise vacations to many exotic destinations and offers a clothing optional cruise aboard the Regal Empress.

Website:	www.allaboardtravel.com
Phone:	800-741-1770 or 239-274-9999
Email:	allaboardtravelfl@earthlink.net
	All Aboard Travel
	12530 World Plaza Lane #1
	Fort Myers, Florida 33907

Index

Index

283